Papatango Theatre Company in partnership with the
Finborough Theatre present

The Papatango Playwriting Festival 2011

⁵OXFINDER

Dawn King

FINBOR...   ...ber 2011

World prem...   ...

FOXFINDER

by Dawn King

Cast in order of appearance

Samuel	**Gyuri Sarossy**
Judith	**Kirsty Besterman**
William	**Tom Byam Shaw**
Sarah	**Becci Gemmell**

The English countryside, on and around the farms of Samuel and Judith Covey and Sarah and Abraham Box.

Director	**Blanche McIntyre**
Designer	**James Perkins**
Lighting Designer	**Gary Bowman**
Sound Designer	**George Dennis**
Casting Director	**Hayley Kaimakliotis**
Assistant Director	**Veronica Quilligan**
Production Manager	**Jane Arnold**
Stage Manager	**George Ransley**
Costume Designer	**Joanna Relf**

The performance lasts approximately ninety minutes.
There will be no interval.

Special Thanks to
Miranda Cass
Jonathan Lane
Jeremy Gold
John and Yvonne Roberts
Chris Roberts (www.thisisuncoated.co.uk)
Image for *Foxfinder* | Garry Lake www.garrylakephotography.com

**Shoreditch
Trust**

Our patrons are respectfully reminded that, in this intimate theatre, any noise such as rustling programmes, talking or the ringing of mobile phones may distract the actors and your fellow audience members.

Kirsty Besterman | Judith

Trained at the Royal Academy of Dramatic Art.

Theatre includes *The Importance of Being Earnest* (Rose Theatre, Kingston), *The Merchant of Venice, Much Ado About Nothing, Holding Fire!, Liberty* (Shakespeare's Globe), *King Lear* (Royal Shakespeare Company), *The Rivals* (Theatre Royal, Bath), *Othello* (Cheek By Jowl), *Amy's View* (Nottingham Playhouse), *Plunder* (Watermill Theatre, Newbury), *Edmond* (Wilton's Music Hall), *Twelfth Night* (Ludlow Theatre Festival), *People Are Stupid: A Political Memoir* (Arcola Theatre) and *Private Lives* (Simply Theatre).

Television includes *Foyle's War*.

Tom Byam Shaw | William

Trained at the Guildhall School of Music and Drama.

Theatre includes *The Tempest* (Theatre Royal Haymarket), *Salome* (Headlong Theatre) and *Les Parents Terribles* (Donmar Warehouse at Trafalgar Studios).

Film includes *Grand Street* (Atlantic Pictures).

Television includes *A Room With A View* and *The Bill*.

Becci Gemmell | Sarah
Trained at Drama Studio London.
Theatre includes *66 Books* (Bush Theatre), *Lark Rise to Candleford* (National Tour), *Eurydice* (Young Vic and National Tour), *F*cked* (Old Red Lion Theatre), *As You Like It* (The Curve, Leicester), *How to Disappear Completely and Never Be Found* (Southwark Playhouse), *Uncertainty* (Latitude Festival), *Mad Funny Just* (Theatre503), *Gleaming Dark* (Trafalgar Studios), *A Midsummer Night's Dream* (Oxford Shakespeare Company), *Winter Anniversary* (The Old Vic 24 Hour Plays), *Much Ado About Nothing* (Guildford Shakespeare Company), *Air Guitar* (Bristol Old Vic Studio) and *Volpone* (Wilton's Music Hall).
Film includes *Red Lights*.
Television includes *Land Girls*, *Home Time*, *Meeting* and *Angel of Death – The Story of Beverly Allitt*.

Gyuri Sarossy | Samuel
At the Finborough Theatre, Gyuri appeared in *Hangover Square* (2008) and *Molière or the League of Hypocrites* (2009).
Trained at the Bristol Old Vic Theatre School.
Other theatre includes *Romeo and Juliet* (Royal Shakespeare Company), *Earthquakes in London* (Headlong Theatre at National Theatre), *Balmoral, Man and Superman, Galileo's Daughter, Don Juan* (The Peter Hall Company), *As You Like It* (Royal Exchange Theatre, Manchester), *The Ragged Trousered Philanthropists* (Liverpool Playhouse and Chichester Festival Theatre), *Twelfth Night, Uncle Vanya* (Donmar Warehouse), *Luther* (National Theatre), *The Hypochondriac* (Almeida Theatre), *Macbeth, Coriolanus* (Shakespeare at The Tobacco Factory), *Rope* (Watermill Theatre, Newbury), *The Promise* (Tricycle Theatre), *The Tempest* (Nuffield Theatre, Southampton), *Romeo and Juliet* (Haymarket Theatre, Leicester), *Simplicity* (Orange Tree Theatre, Richmond) and *A Christmas Carol* (Bristol Old Vic).
Film includes *Another Life, After Death, Sheepish, Spirit of the Fox* and *Jean*.
Television includes *Einstein and Eddington, Tchaikovsky, Judge John Deed, Egypt, The Bill, Holby City, EastEnders, Casualty, Doctors, Blue Dove, Belfry Witches, Up Rising* and *Kavanagh QC*.
Radio includes *Getting Nowhere Fast* and *Twenty Cigarettes*.
Forthcoming productions include playing Leo in *Design For Living* at Salisbury Playhouse in January.

Dawn King | Playwright
Playwright Dawn King was one of ten writers from across the UK chosen for the BBC Writersroom 10 scheme, a prestigious mentoring and support programme. Through this she is developing a new play with West Yorkshire Playhouse. She is also currently writing *My One and Only*, an afternoon play for BBC Radio 4. Her episode of horror series *The Man in Black* will broadcast on BBC Radio 4 Extra later this year. Previous radio work includes afternoon play *28* and episodes for the first and second series of science fiction drama *Planet B* for BBC Radio 7. She was made co-series leader for the third series. Her recent theatre includes *Water Sculptures/Zoo* double bill (Union Theatre), *Face Value* (Stephen Joseph Theatre, Scarborough), *The Bitches' Ball* (Hoxton Hall, National Tour and Assembly Rooms, Edinburgh), and *Doghead Boy and Sharkmouth Go To Ikea* (The Junction, Cambridge). Previous work has received performances, workshops and readings at the Royal Court Theatre, Soho Theatre, Hampstead Theatre, Theatre503, Arcola Theatre, Old Red Lion Theatre, Etcetera Theatre, the Latitude Festival, Resonance FM and The Union Theatre. Dawn was a member of both the Soho Theatre and Royal Court Theatre Young Writers' Programmes and holds an MA distinction in Writing for Performance from Goldsmiths University, London. www.dawn-king.com

Blanche McIntyre | Director
At the Finborough Theatre, Blanche was the the winner of the first Leverhulme Bursary for Emerging Theatre Directors, and was Director in Residence at the National Theatre Studio and the Finborough Theatre in 2009. Direction at the Finborough Theatre includes *Molière or the League of Hypocrites* (2009), *Accolade* (2010) and staged readings for *Vibrant – A Festival of Finborough Playwrights* including *Green* (2009), *Rock Paper Scissors* (2010), *The Voice of Scotland* (2010) and *In World* (2011).
Other directing includes *When Did You Last See My Mother?* (Trafalgar Studios), *Pinching For My Soul* (Focus Theatre, Dublin), *Robin Hood* (Latitude Festival), *Open Heart Surgery* (Soho Theatre and Southwark Playhouse), *Wuthering Heights* (National Tour), *The Revenger's Tragedy* (BAC), *The Master and Margarita* (Greenwich Playhouse), *Three Hours After Marriage* (Union Theatre), *Doctor Faustus*, *The Devil Is An Ass* and *The Strange Case of Dr Jekyll and Mr Hyde as Told to Carl Jung by an Inmate of Broadmoor Asylum* (White Bear Theatre), *Cressida* and *The Invention of Love* (Edinburgh Festival) and *Prometheus Bound* (Burton Taylor Theatre, Oxford). She was also Associate Director at Out of Joint in 2010, working on *The Big Fellah* (Out of Joint 2010 and 2011 tours). Blanche also works as a writer and librettist.

James Perkins | Designer
At the Finborough Theatre, James designed *Trying* (2009).
James is one third of theatre collective paper/scissors/stone and Resident Designer for Charles Court Opera. Design highlights include *The Girl in the Yellow Dress* (Salisbury Playhouse), *Matters of Life and Death* (UK Contemporary Dance Tour), *Many Moons* (Theatre503), *Stockwell* (Tricycle Theatre), *The Marriage of Figaro*

(Wilton's Music Hall), *Saraband* (Jermyn Street Theatre), *Girls and Dolls, Colourings* (Old Red Lion Theatre), *Orpheus, Troy Boy* (National Tour), *Iolanthe, The Way Through The Woods* (Pleasance, London), *The Pirates of Penzance, HMS Pinafore* (Buxton Opera House), *The Barber* (Greenwich Theatre), *The Faerie Queen* (Lilian Baylis Theatre) and *The Wonder* (BAC).

Gary Bowman | Lighting Designer
At the Finborough Theatre, Gary was Lighting Designer for *Apart from George* (2009) and *S-27* (2009).
Trained at Bristol Old Vic Theatre School.
Lighting designs include *Once on this Island* (Cockpit Theatre), *Jest End* (Leicester Square Theatre and Jermyn Street Theatre), *Gotcha* (Riverside Studios), *A Moment of Silence, Ordinary Lads* (Etcetera Theatre), *Miss Julie* (Attic Theatre), *Stuff, Leopoldville* (Tristan Bates Theatre), *Angel, The Muse* (Pleasance London) and *So Jest End* (Charing Cross Theatre).
He has also worked as a production electrician in both New York and the West End on productions including *Buddy* (Duchess Theatre), *The Lover* and *The Collection, Dickens Un-Plugged* (Comedy Theatre), *Wicked* (Apollo Victoria Theatre), *Chicago* (Cambridge Theatre), *Rock of Ages* (Shaftesbury Theatre) and as Deputy Chief Electrician at the Donmar Warehouse.
Gary was nominated for a 2011 Off West End Award for Best Lighting Designer for *Gotcha* at Riverside Studios.

George Dennis | Sound Designer
Sound designs at the Finborough Theatre include *The December Man/L'homme de Décembre*, part of *Vibrant – A Festival of Finborough Playwrights* (2010), *Generous, A Day At The Racists, You May Go Now* (all 2010), Resident Sound Designer for *Vibrant – An Anniversary Festival of Finborough Playwrights* (2010), *Me and Juliet* (2010), *The Goodnight Bird* (2011) and *Portraits* (2011).
Trained at the University of Manchester with an MA in Music.
Theatre includes *The York Realist, The Sleepers Den* (Riverside Studios), *Studies For a Portrait* (King's Head Theatre), *Us* (Hampstead Theatre Studio) and *The York Realist* (Riverside Studios). George has won international acclaim for his composition work, taking first prize in *Música Viva Competition*, Lisbon, in 2008, and a prize in *Concurso VI*, Seville, in 2008

Joanna Relf | Costume Designer
Trained at the Royal Welsh College of Music and Drama. Costume Design includes *Medea* (Bridewell Theatre), *Coriolanus* (Brockley Jack Theatre), *Odette* (Bridewell Theatre), *Smile, Launderette* (National Film and Television School) and *Reaching Higher* (Tornado Films and BBC Wales). She has also worked as a Costume Assistant and Maker on *The Madness of King George* (Devonshire Park Theatre), *Dick Whittington and His Cat, Twisted Tales, 1984, Saved, Aladdin* (Lyric Theatre, Hammersmith) and *Ghost Stories* (Duke of York's Theatre). She also spent a year at Angels the Costumiers working on productions such as *Quantum of Solace, The Imaginarium of Dr Parnassus* and *The Edge of Love*.

PAPAtango

Papatango was founded by Matt Roberts, George Turvey and Sam Donovan in 2007. The company's mission is to find the best and brightest new talent in the UK with an absolute commitment to bring their work to the stage. 2009 saw the launch of their first Papatango New Writing Competition, which each year has gone from strength to strength.

Now in its new home – the multi-award-winning Finborough Theatre – this year's competition received over 600 entries from all over the UK. This year's judges included Con O'Neill (actor), Catherine Johnson (playwright), Matt Charman (playwright), Colin Barr (BBC director and producer), Tamara Harvey (director), Ruth Carney (director), Neil McPherson (Artistic Director of the Finborough Theatre), Van Badham (Literary Manager of the Finborough Theatre) and Tanya Tillett (Literary Agent, The Rod Hall Agency).

papatango.theatre@gmail.com
www.papatango.co.uk

Online
For up to date news join us on Facebook, Twitter or email papatango.theatre@gmail.com to join our mailing list.

Co-Artistic Directors
Sam Donovan
Matt Roberts
George Turvey

Associate Artistic Director
Bruce Guthrie

Patrons
Howard Davies CBE
Jeremy Gold
David Suchet OBE
Zoe Wanamaker CBE
Andrew Welch

Artistic Advisors
Colin Barr
Ruth Carney
Matt Charman
Tamara Harvey
Catherine Johnson
Jeremy Kingston
Con O'Neil
Tanya Tillett

The three runners up in the Competition will also be produced for a week long run at the Finborough Theatre this month:

Tuesday, 6 December – Sunday, 11 December 2011
Through The Night
by Matt Morrison
Directed by Matt Grinter

Tuesday, 13 December – Sunday, 18 December 2011
Rigor Mortis
by Carol Vine
Directed by Kate Budgen

Monday, 19 December – Friday, 23 December 2011
Crush
by Rob Young
Directed by Laura Casey

FINBOROUGH | THEATRE

The Stage's Fringe Theatre of the Year

**Winner – London Theatre Reviews'
Empty Space Peter Brook Award 2010**

'One of the most stimulating venues in
London, fielding a programme that is a
bold mix of trenchant, politically thought-
provoking new drama and shrewdly
chosen revivals of neglected works from
the past.' *The Independent*

'A disproportionately valuable component
of the London theatre ecology. Its
programme combines new writing and
revivals, in selections intelligent and
audacious.' *Financial Times*

'A blazing beacon of intelligent endeavour, nurturing new writers
while finding and reviving neglected curiosities from home and
abroad.' *Daily Telegraph*

Founded in 1980, the multi-award-winning Finborough Theatre presents
plays and music theatre, concentrated exclusively on new writing and
genuine rediscoveries from the 19th and 20th centuries. We offer a
stimulating and inclusive programme, appealing to theatregoers of all
generations and from a broad spectrum of the population. Behind the
scenes, we continue to discover and develop a new generation of theatre
makers – through our vibrant Literary Department, our internship
programme, our Resident Assistant Director Programme, and our partnership
with the National Theatre Studio – the Leverhulme Bursary for Emerging
Directors.

Despite remaining completely unfunded, the Finborough Theatre has an
unparalleled track record of attracting the finest creative talent, as well as
discovering new playwrights who go on to become leading voices in British
theatre. Under Artistic Director Neil McPherson, it has discovered some of the
UK's most exciting new playwrights including Laura Wade, James Graham, Mike
Bartlett, Sarah Grochala, Jack Thorne, Simon Vinnicombe, Alexandra Wood, Al
Smith, Nicholas de Jongh and Anders Lustgarten.

Artists working at the theatre in the 1980s included Clive Barker, Rory
Bremner, Nica Burns, Kathy Burke, Ken Campbell, Jane Horrocks and Claire
Dowie. In the 1990s, the Finborough Theatre became known for new writing
including Naomi Wallace's first play *The War Boys*; Rachel Weisz in David
Farr's *Neville Southall's Washbag*; four plays by Anthony Neilson including
Penetrator and *The Censor*, both of which transferred to the Royal Court
Theatre; and new plays by Tony Marchant, David Eldridge, Mark Ravenhill
and Phil Willmott. New writing development included a number of works that
went on to become modern classics including Mark Ravenhill's *Shopping and
F***king*, Conor McPherson's *This Lime Tree Bower*, Naomi Wallace's
Slaughter City and Martin McDonagh's *The Pillowman*.

Since 2000, new British plays have included Laura Wade's London debut – *Young Emma*, commissioned for the Finborough Theatre; James Graham's *Albert's Boy* with Victor Spinetti; Sarah Grochala's *S27*; Peter Nichols' *Lingua Franca*, which transferred Off-Broadway; and Joy Wilkinson's *Fair*; Nicholas de Jongh's *Plague Over England*; and Jack Thorne's *Fanny and Faggot*, all of which transferred to the West End. The late Miriam Karlin made her last stage appearance in *Many Roads to Paradise* in 2008. Many of the Finborough Theatre's new plays have been published and are on sale from our website.

UK premieres of foreign plays have included Brad Fraser's *Wolfboy*; Lanford Wilson's *Sympathetic Magic*; Larry Kramer's *The Destiny of Me*; Tennessee Williams' *Something Cloudy, Something Clear*; the English premiere of Robert McLellan's Scots language classic, *Jamie the Saxt*; and three West End transfers – Frank McGuinness' *Gates of Gold* with William Gaunt and John Bennett, Joe DiPietro's *F***ing Men* and Craig Higginson's *Dream of the Dog* with Janet Suzman.

Rediscoveries of neglected work have included the first London revivals of Rolf Hochhuth's *Soldiers* and *The Representative*; both parts of Keith Dewhurst's *Lark Rise to Candleford*; *The Women's War*, an evening of original suffragette plays; *Etta Jenks* with Clarke Peters and Daniela Nardini; Noël Coward's first play, *The Rat Trap*; Charles Wood's *Jingo* with Susannah Harker; Emlyn Williams' *Accolade* with Aden Gillett and Graham Seed; and Lennox Robinson's *Drama at Inish* with Celia Imrie and Paul O'Grady.

Music Theatre has included the new (premieres from Grant Olding, Charles Miller, Michael John LaChuisa, Adam Guettel, Andrew Lippa and Adam Gwon's *Ordinary Days* which transferred to the West End) and the old (the UK premiere of Rodgers and Hammerstein's *State Fair* which also transferred to the West End, and the acclaimed Celebrating British Music Theatre series, reviving forgotten British musicals).

The Finborough Theatre won *London Theatre Reviews'* Empty Space Peter Brook Award in 2010, the Empty Space Peter Brook Award's Dan Crawford Pub Theatre Award in 2005 and 2008, the Empty Space Peter Brook Mark Marvin Award in 2004, and four awards in the inaugural 2011 Off West End Awards. It is the only theatre without public funding to be awarded the Pearson Playwriting Award bursary for writers Chris Lee in 2000, Laura Wade in 2005 (who also went on to win the Critics' Circle Theatre Award for Most Promising Playwright, the George Devine Award and an Olivier Award nomination), for James Graham in 2006, for Al Smith in 2007, for Anders Lustgarten in 2009 and Simon Vinnicombe in 2010. Three bursary holders (Laura Wade, James Graham and Anders Lustgarten) have also won the Catherine Johnson Award for Best Play written by a bursary holder. Artistic Director Neil McPherson won the Best Artistic Director award from *Fringe Report* in 2009 and from the Off West End Awards in 2011, and a Writers' Guild Award for the Encouragement of New Writing in 2010.

www.finboroughtheatre.co.uk

FINBOROUGH | THEATRE

118 Finborough Road, London SW10 9ED
admin@finboroughtheatre.co.uk
www.finboroughtheatre.co.uk

The Leverhulme Bursary for Emerging Directors is a partnership
between the National Theatre Studio and the Finborough Theatre,
supported by The Leverhulme Trust.

The Finborough Theatre is a member of the Independent Theatre
Council, Musical Theatre Matters UK (MTM:UK) and The Earl's Court
Society www.earlscourtsociety.org.uk

Ecovenue is a European Regional Development Fund backed three-year
initiative of The Theatres Trust, aiming to improve the environmental
sustainability of 48 small to medium-sized performing arts spaces across
London. www.ecovenue.org.uk

Online
Join us at Facebook, Twitter, MySpace and YouTube.

Mailing

Email admin@finboroughtheatre.co.uk or give your details to our Box Office staff to join our free email list. If you would like to be sent a free season leaflet every three months, just include your postal address and postcode.

Feedback

We welcome your comments, complaints and suggestions. Write to Finborough Theatre, 118 Finborough Road, London SW10 9ED or email us at admin@finboroughtheatre.co.uk

Friends

The Finborough Theatre is a registered charity. We receive no public funding, and rely solely on the support of our audiences. Please do consider supporting us by becoming a member of our Friends of the Finborough Theatre scheme. There are four categories of Friends, each offering a wide range of benefits.

Brandon Thomas Friends – Bruce Cleave. Mike Lewendon.
Richard Tauber Friends – Harry MacAuslan. Brian Smith.
William Terriss Friends – Leo and Janet Liebster. Philip Hooker.
Peter Lobl. Bhagat Sharma. Thurloe and Lyndhurst LLP. Jon Sedmak.

FOXFINDER

Dawn King

Acknowledgements

With grateful thanks to everyone who helped, including:

The Peggy Ramsay Foundation for their financial support.

Paul Jenkins, who first helped me to see foxes.

Will Davis, Tom Mansfield, Terry Saunders, Julia Mills and Matt Connell for their advice and support.

Papatango Theatre Company and the Finborough Theatre.

Mum, Dad and my husband Mr Richard George, for everything.

Dawn King

Characters

WILLIAM BLOOR, *a foxfinder, nineteen*
SAMUEL COVEY, *a farmer, late thirties*
JUDITH COVEY, *his wife, attractive, early thirties*
SARAH BOX, *a neighbour, early thirties*

This text went to press before the end of rehearsals and so may differ slightly from the play as performed.

1

A farmhouse kitchen. Minimal decoration, scrupulously clean.
SAMUEL and JUDITH are sitting at the table. Both are in their
Sunday best – neat, plain clothes of timeless appearance. It is
raining heavily outside.

SAMUEL. Went up the top this morning. I reckon half that
wheat has had it.

JUDITH. It might recover.

SAMUEL. Not if this weather keeps on.

Pause.

And east-gate field… waste of seed that was. It's like a bog.

JUDITH. We might get something from it. Better than nothing.

SAMUEL. I planted it too early. You can say that.

JUDITH. We don't know yet, do we? The rain could stop
tomorrow.

Pause.

There's a good crop of leeks coming.

SAMUEL. Huh. I wouldn't call it good.

Pause. The rain batters against the windows.

Listen to it. It's stupid travelling on a day like this.

JUDITH. He'll be soaked. And frozen.

SAMUEL. Aye.

Pause.

Show me the letter again.

JUDITH *holds out a letter.* SAMUEL *takes it. Looks at it.*

Fancy hand he's got. Very nice.

JUDITH. It's an honour having one of them stay. Everyone says that.

SAMUEL. Huh. 'Investigating the area.' What does that mean?

JUDITH. I don't know.

Pause.

SAMUEL. I don't see why it has to be us.

JUDITH. It doesn't say.

SAMUEL. There are plenty others as has more room. In 'the area'.

JUDITH. Yes, but he –

SAMUEL. He should be staying at the big house.

JUDITH. He asked to stay here.

SAMUEL. Aye. He did.

Pause.

If there was something going on, on our land, I'd know. Don't I know my own land? I'm out there all times of day and night and I've seen nothing. You've seen nothing. The men have seen nothing. There is nothing.

JUDITH. They're clever. They hide, that's what people say.

SAMUEL. I'd *know.*

JUDITH *nods. Pause.*

He's heard something. Must have.

JUDITH. What?

SAMUEL. Someone's been telling tall tales, I bet.

JUDITH. Don't say that. Who'd do that?

SAMUEL. Could be anyone.

JUDITH *looks worried.*

JUDITH. No. That can't be it.

SAMUEL. I'll ask him when he gets here.

JUDITH. Don't you dare! If someone's said something, you'll just make it worse!

Pause.

SAMUEL. Fine. Let him waste his time chasing rumours. I'll say nothing.

Pause.

JUDITH. What time is it?

SAMUEL. Twenty past. He's late.

JUDITH. He'll be here soon.

SAMUEL. You said that an hour ago.

JUDITH. Maybe the roads are flooded.

SAMUEL. Aye, I reckon. And the bridge will be out before long.

JUDITH. It's no good, Sam, you'll have to go out looking for him.

SAMUEL. I'll not. I've got animals need feeding. They won't wait.

JUDITH. What if he's lost?

SAMUEL. Then he won't come. So I can get on.

He gets up.

JUDITH. No, you're not leaving me to meet him alone!

SAMUEL. All right.

SAMUEL *sits back down.*

JUDITH. When hc comes, you can't be rude to him. Be polite. Promise me.

SAMUEL. He'll have to take us as he finds us, won't he?

JUDITH. Sam!

A knock at the door. JUDITH *jumps up.*

It's him.

She hesitates.

SAMUEL. Open it then.

JUDITH. I can't.

SAMUEL *opens the door.* WILLIAM *stands there. He wears a black greatcoat and wide-brimmed hat. He carries several heavy bags.*

SAMUEL. William Bloor, is it?

WILLIAM. Yes.

SAMUEL. I'm Sam Covey. Come in.

WILLIAM *smiles apologetically.*

WILLIAM. Not yet.

SAMUEL. Oh.

WILLIAM. Is the lady of the house present?

SAMUEL. Judith!

JUDITH *goes to the door.*

WILLIAM. Are you Judith Covey, Mrs?

JUDITH. Yes, that's right.

She puts out her hand.

Come in. You must be freezing!

WILLIAM. And you're Samuel Covey, Mr.

SAMUEL. I am. I said that.

WILLIAM. Do you have any identification?

SAMUEL. Excuse me?

WILLIAM. I need to see some identification. For both of you. Please.

JUDITH*'s hand droops.*

JUDITH. Uhm.

JUDITH goes over to a chest of drawers and starts rummaging. WILLIAM stands in the rain, holding his bags.

SAMUEL. A funny way of greeting people.

WILLIAM. I'm sorry, but you could be anyone.

SAMUEL. You think we've chucked the real Coveys down the well or something?

WILLIAM. I don't know. Have you?

JUDITH shows him some papers. He nods. Finally he comes inside and puts the bags down.

You'll have to excuse me for seeming rude. Judith.

He offers his hand. She shakes it. He smiles.

Samuel.

SAMUEL shakes his offered hand.

Thank you for letting me stay. We appreciate your help in this matter.

Pause.

JUDITH. It's no trouble. We're glad to have you. We don't get many visitors. I'll put the kettle on.

WILLIAM. If you don't mind, I'll put my bags away first.

JUDITH. Oh. Yes. The room's quite small, I'm afraid.

WILLIAM. I'm sure it will be more than adequate.

SAMUEL bends to pick up his bags.

No, I'll take those, if you don't mind.

SAMUEL steps back.

JUDITH. It's this way.

JUDITH goes out. WILLIAM picks up the bags, nods to SAMUEL, and follows her.

2

WILLIAM, *now dressed in a plain shirt, black waistcoat and trousers, sits with* JUDITH *and* SAMUEL *at the table. The remains of a meal of soup and bread are in front of him.*

WILLIAM. Thank you. That was delicious.

JUDITH. Will you have a cider to finish off? Or we've got beer?

WILLIAM. No –

JUDITH. Or tea? Coffee?

WILLIAM. – thank you. No.

JUDITH. I'll get these.

JUDITH *gets up and clears* WILLIAM'*s plate and bowl away.* WILLIAM *brushes the table free of crumbs. He gets out a notebook and unfolds a map on the table.* SAMUEL *watches him.*

WILLIAM. I just need to ask you a few questions.

SAMUEL. Now? Can't it wait till morning?

WILLIAM. It won't take long.

JUDITH *sits back down.*

The farm is sixty acres?

SAMUEL. Aye.

WILLIAM *makes a note.*

WILLIAM. And what kind of animals do you have here?

JUDITH. Do you mean… because we've not seen any.

WILLIAM. I mean, simply, what kind of animals does the farm have?

SAMUEL. A few cows, pigs, some chickens. That's it.

WILLIAM. This is an arable farm.

SAMUEL. Yes.

WILLIAM. What about pets?

JUDITH. We had a cat but it ran off.

>WILLIAM *makes a note.*

>Is that important?

WILLIAM. A missing cat as a single, isolated incident is not important.

JUDITH....Oh.

WILLIAM. When did this happen?

JUDITH. March.

>WILLIAM *points to the map.*

WILLIAM. This is the boundary line we have for your property. Is it correct?

SAMUEL. Uh. Looks it.

WILLIAM. It is correct?

SAMUEL. Yes.

WILLIAM. And this land belongs to David Johnson, Mr.

SAMUEL. Yes.

WILLIAM. And this to Abraham Box, Mr.

SAMUEL. It says that on the map already.

WILLIAM. I'm checking my facts. What's this?

JUDITH. That's the woods.

WILLIAM. Woods? Mature trees, young trees... bushes?

SAMUEL. Aah... yes.

WILLIAM. Which?

SAMUEL. Both.

WILLIAM. Pardon?

SAMUEL. All. I mean.

WILLIAM. And who does that belong to?

SAMUEL. Well. No one.

WILLIAM *makes notes*.

WILLIAM. Have you seen pheasants on your property?

SAMUEL. Yes. Johnson raises them to hunt. They fly over the fence.

WILLIAM. What about deer. Have you seen deer on your property?

SAMUEL. Ahh…

JUDITH. No, not very often.

WILLIAM. So your answer is yes?

JUDITH. Yes.

WILLIAM. Ducks. Have you seen ducks, either flying overhead, or on the land?

JUDITH. Uhm…

SAMUEL. No.

WILLIAM. You've never seen ducks here?

SAMUEL. We see ducks, but we don't have ducks here.

WILLIAM. So the answer is yes. You have seen ducks. Flying overhead, or on the land?

SAMUEL *turns away, annoyed*.

JUDITH. Both.

WILLIAM. Have you seen more ducks flying or more ducks on the land, speaking generally?

JUDITH. Uh. Flying.

WILLIAM *makes notes*.

WILLIAM. Badgers?

SAMUEL. Yes. In the thirty-seven years I've lived here, I have seen a badger.

WILLIAM. Samuel, these questions are simply to help me get an idea of the situation here.

SAMUEL. There is no situation here.

WILLIAM. I sincerely hope not. Now, could you both think very hard please before answering this next question. Would you say that the frequency with which you've seen these birds and animals – pheasant, deer, duck, badger – has been more or less in the past year?

They think.

SAMUEL. The same. Not more, not less.

JUDITH *nods agreement*. WILLIAM *makes a note*.

WILLIAM. That's very useful. Thank you.

JUDITH. Aren't you going to ask us… about…

WILLIAM. No.

Long pause. WILLIAM *looks at the map, and his notes*.

Samuel, my notes tell me that the farm is not on target to meet its quota for this year.

SAMUEL *frowns*.

SAMUEL. Aye.

WILLIAM. So far, you've produced less than two thirds of what you did last year.

JUDITH. It can't be that bad.

WILLIAM. Look at the figures.

JUDITH. We'll make it up with the winter harvest.

WILLIAM. Frankly, that's impossible.

SAMUEL. That's why you came here.

WILLIAM. I'm here to help you.

SAMUEL. Huh.

WILLIAM. We take the security of England's food supply very seriously. There's little margin for error. If one farm falls behind, another has to pick up the slack. Or people go hungry.

SAMUEL. We know that.

WILLIAM. And a country marches on her stomach, Samuel. Without food, we're defenceless. Open to exploitation by any foreign power.

SAMUEL. Abe's behind as well.

WILLIAM. Abraham Box won't make his quota?

WILLIAM pages through his notes. JUDITH shoots SAMUEL a warning look.

The Box farm is almost on target. Are you saying that their winter harvest will be low?

SAMUEL. Half his fields are underwater. What do you expect?

WILLIAM. England expects that every citizen will do their duty.

JUDITH. Yes, of course.

WILLIAM. What about your other neighbours? Do you know anything about them?

SAMUEL. My great-grandfather built this farm. Does it say that in your notes?

WILLIAM. Yes. An impressive heritage. Do you know anything about –

JUDITH. Don't take our farm.

SAMUEL. Jude, be quiet.

JUDITH. We've had a bad year. The flooding. And the leaf blight. And… our son.

WILLIAM. Your son?

JUDITH. He died.

Pause. WILLIAM looks in his notes.

WILLIAM. Your son Daniel, aged four?

JUDITH. Yes.

WILLIAM. You didn't notify us.

JUDITH. I. No. I'm sorry. We… we forgot.

WILLIAM. I see.

JUDITH. It was a bad time.

WILLIAM. I'm very sorry for your loss.

JUDITH. Thank you.

WILLIAM. And you don't have any other children.

JUDITH. No.

SAMUEL *stands up.*

SAMUEL. I've to lock up. It's late.

WILLIAM. I know this is difficult but I have to ask. When did Daniel die?

JUDITH. March.

SAMUEL *leaves the room.*

WILLIAM. And… how?

JUDITH. An accident.

WILLIAM *writes notes.*

Mr Bloor… I…

WILLIAM. Call me William.

JUDITH. William. My husband… he's been ill. He…

WILLIAM. He has? I'm sorry to hear that. What form of illness?

JUDITH *frowns.*

JUDITH. Sam's fine now. We're doing fine.

WILLIAM. Judith, this farm has everything it could possibly need in terms of workers, land and equipment. And yet, you have failed to meet the targets set for you. The question we must ask is 'Why?'

JUDITH. Bad luck.

WILLIAM. There's no such thing.

JUDITH *doesn't know what to say.*

You're uncomfortable with my presence here. You obviously want me to leave.

JUDITH. Well no, I...

WILLIAM. Is there something you'd like to confess?

JUDITH *is shocked.*

JUDITH. No! I just meant. That. Sam needs quiet and... I'd like you to get done here as soon as possible, for his sake, is all I meant.

WILLIAM. And for his sake, for your sake, and the sake of our country, I'll do my job. Is that clear?

JUDITH *nods.*

Now, tell me, when did Samuel fall ill?

JUDITH. March.

WILLIAM *makes a note.*

WILLIAM. And his symptoms?

JUDITH. It was flu. Bad flu. Left him weak as a kitten. He couldn't work for weeks.

WILLIAM *looks at* JUDITH. *She is lying and he knows it.*

WILLIAM. I see.

He writes more notes. JUDITH *stands there looking increasingly uncomfortable.*

Eventually WILLIAM *looks up.*

Thank you, Judith. That's given me a lot to think about.

Dismissed, JUDITH *leaves.*

3

SAMUEL *and* JUDITH*'s bedroom.* SAMUEL *is sitting on the bed, staring into space.*

JUDITH *comes in. She sits on the bed.*

JUDITH. Sam?

Pause.

SAMUEL. He's here because we're behind.

JUDITH. He didn't say that.

SAMUEL. He's here because we're behind. And we're behind because of me.

JUDITH. It wasn't your fault.

SAMUEL. You never should have married me.

JUDITH. Sam, don't.

Pause.

We'll be all right. They won't take the farm because of one bad year.

SAMUEL. They took Billy Gunn's place and gave it to Johnson.

JUDITH. That's different. He was old. And… he had no heir.

SAMUEL. Aye.

Pause.

JUDITH *takes* SAMUEL*'s hand.*

JUDITH. Sam, the quickest way to get rid of him is to answer all his questions and show him there's nothing wrong here.

SAMUEL. Huh.

JUDITH. Once he's gone we can think about the future. Next year's going to be better.

SAMUEL. It could hardly be worse.

She puts her arms around him.

JUDITH. We'll be all right, you'll see.

He nods.

SAMUEL. I don't deserve you.

JUDITH. Don't be stupid.

She kisses him. He kisses her back. She presses, trying to make the kiss more passionate. He pulls away gently.

SAMUEL. I... it's late.

JUDITH *nods, resigned. They start getting ready for bed.*

WILLIAM *is in the spare bedroom, on the other side of the wall.*

His travelling coat is hanging on the back of a wardrobe, dripping. His bags sit at the foot of the single bed.

WILLIAM. The Personal Journal of William Bloor. Monday. Arrive at the farm of Mr and Mrs Samuel Covey. During the journey here, I noted several birds circling overhead in a suspicious manner. Due to the rain, was unable to make an accurate identification, but was in any case glad to reach cover. The Covey's farm is very remote; prime territory for an infestation. It is late, I am tired and this room unusually cold, but this only serves to drive any distractions from my mind and remind me of the seriousness of my mission. My preliminary questioning, which took place after an excellent leek and potato soup provided by Judith, and my own first impressions lead me to some immediate conclusions – 1: The death of the Covey's only child Daniel, Samuel's illness, disappearance of cat and downturn in the farm's productivity all occurred in March of this year. 2: Judith is attempting to be friendly but is clearly afraid of me. Despite this, she challenged my presence here and came close to telling me to

leave. An unusually brave woman, or a desperate one?
3: Death of son was not reported. Why? 4: Samuel tense
almost to the point of aggression. Parental grief combined
with stress, possibly, but it could be something more.

WILLIAM *puts his ear to the wall separating his room from*
JUDITH *and* SAMUEL*'s. There is silence from the room –*
they are lying still. WILLIAM *makes a note in his notebook.*

WILLIAM *opens one of his bags and takes out a shirt. He*
opens the door of the wardrobe and is hanging the shirt up
when he sees something inside the wardrobe.

He pulls it out. It's a child's toy, a wooden horse on wheels,
very dusty.

4

Morning. JUDITH *is in the kitchen pouring a cup of coffee for*
SARAH, *a neighbour.*

JUDITH. It's not you he's investigating.

SARAH. If he thinks he's found something here, he'll be
knocking on our door next. Stands to reason.

JUDITH. He won't find anything if there's nothing to find.

SARAH. If?

JUDITH. You don't think we've got them, do you?

SARAH. No. Definitely not.

JUDITH. Then he won't find anything. He'll be gone in a few
days.

SARAH. I hope so.

Pause. SARAH *looks at* JUDITH.

How've you been? You look tired.

JUDITH. I am. Feeling… like this, every day… it's exhausting.

Pause.

SARAH. I don't know how you cope.

JUDITH. One of us has to be the strong one.

SARAH. At least Sam's out of bed now.

JUDITH. He is. He's doing much better.

SARAH. What about…

JUDITH. Well. No. He keeps saying he's tired. Or he stays up until I'm asleep.

SARAH. You've got to keep trying.

JUDITH. I don't want to push him. Might make it worse.

SARAH. It's been half a year, Jude. More.

JUDITH. He needs time.

SARAH. What about what you need?

Pause.

If *he* finds out you're not… it'll count against you.

JUDITH. How's he going to find out? I'll not tell him.

SARAH. And Sam…

JUDITH. Sam won't even talk to me about it.

SARAH *nods.*

SARAH. What's he like?

JUDITH. Young. Thin. Too thin.

SARAH. They raise them up like monks. And they live like monks too. No women. No drinking. No nothing.

JUDITH. Oh. I offered him a drink last night.

SARAH. Be careful! You don't want him thinking you're a couple of lushes!

JUDITH. I asked him if he wanted a cider, that's all. We didn't have any.

SARAH. Good. He's dangerous. One word from him and that's it, you're out.

JUDITH. He says he's here to help us.

SARAH. Jude... last time I went up to town with Abe... someone gave me this.

She pulls out a crudely printed pamphlet entitled 'Foxes – Not Our Enemy'. She gives it to JUDITH.

JUDITH. Good God! Why did you bring this here when I've got him under my roof?

SARAH. It says the fox is almost extinct in England.

JUDITH. That's wonderful!

SARAH. Is it?

JUDITH. Of course!

SARAH. If the foxes are gone, things should be getting better. Do you think things are getting better?

JUDITH. I... I don't want this, Sarah.

SARAH. You need to read it.

JUDITH. No! Take it back. I've got enough to worry about.

JUDITH *pushes the pamphlet back into* SARAH*'s hands.*

WILLIAM *appears in the doorway. He is behind* SARAH *so he can't see what she's holding.*

Mr Bloor. Good morning.

WILLIAM. William, please, call me William. Good morning...?

SARAH *pushes the pamphlet into her pocket.*

JUDITH. This is Sarah. Sarah, this is Mr William Bloor.

WILLIAM. Sarah Box, Mrs. Married to Abraham. Children; Nathaniel and Rebecca. Your farm is west of here, I think?

SARAH. That's right.

WILLIAM *holds out his hand, smiling*. SARAH *shakes it*.

I… I was just saying to Judith. She's lucky, having a foxfinder stay. It's a real privilege.

WILLIAM. I'm sure Judith would rather I wasn't here getting under her feet.

JUDITH. No. I mean. I'm glad you're here. You're trying to help us.

WILLIAM. Indeed I am.

JUDITH. You've missed breakfast.

WILLIAM. Yes. I had a rather restless night. And then I overslept. Not like me at all.

JUDITH. Something wrong with the room?

WILLIAM. No, no, it's fine.

JUDITH. Sit down. I'll make you something.

WILLIAM. Do you have a piece of bread?

JUDITH. Uh…

WILLIAM. I'll take it with me.

JUDITH *gives* WILLIAM *bread. He puts it in his bag.*

Goodbye then, ladies.

WILLIAM *leaves the house*.

SARAH. Oh –

JUDITH. Ssh!

JUDITH *goes to the door.*

He's gone.

SARAH. Do you think he heard what I said?

JUDITH. I don't know. No. No I don't think so.

SARAH. You said he'd already gone out!

JUDITH. I thought he had!

SARAH. You should have checked his room!

JUDITH. I listened outside the door. How was I supposed to know?

Pause.

SARAH. If he heard me...

JUDITH. He didn't.

SARAH. I'm going home.

JUDITH. Sarah...

SARAH. What?

JUDITH. He knows that you and Abe are going to be low this harvest. Sam said something about it.

SARAH. It's not Sam's business to talk to him about our farm!

JUDITH. He didn't mean to –

SARAH. For God's sake! We don't need you giving him reasons to investigate us.

JUDITH. No. I know.

SARAH. I'm going. I need to talk to Abe.

JUDITH. I'm sorry.

SARAH. Just be careful what you say around him.

JUDITH. I will.

She leaves the pamphlet on the table and goes out.

Don't leave that here. Sarah!

JUDITH *looks at the pamphlet on the table as it if were a dangerous animal. Eventually, she picks it up, folds it small and shoves it into her pocket.*

5

WILLIAM *is crouching in a muddy field. He stares intently at something in the distance.*

SAMUEL *appears at the edge of the field. He looks at* WILLIAM.

SAMUEL. Uh.

WILLIAM. Samuel. Good morning.

SAMUEL. It's one o' clock.

WILLIAM. Ah. Good afternoon then.

    Pause.

SAMUEL. What're you looking at?

WILLIAM. Those woods.

SAMUEL. Oh.

    They both stare at the trees.

    Did you see summat?

WILLIAM. I found…

    WILLIAM *reaches into his bag and pulls out a small animal skull.*

    …this. It was lying in the next field, with its empty eye sockets pointing directly at those trees. Directly. As if it were staring. Do you see?

SAMUEL. It's a rabbit skull.

WILLIAM. It's a message.

    SAMUEL *is totally nonplussed.*

SAMUEL. What?

WILLIAM. The red beast preys on the rabbit. Which makes the rabbit our ally.

SAMUEL. Does it? Because they eat half my crops every year.

WILLIAM. I think the rabbits on your farm could be trying to warn us.

SAMUEL. You're saying this rabbit... it decided to lie down and die, pointing at that tree, because it knew that you'd come along and find it?

WILLIAM. Nature is full of symbols, Samuel. You just have to know how to interpret them.

SAMUEL. Huh.

WILLIAM. This field, this farm... this entire country is a battleground between the forces of civilisation and the forces of nature. If we lose, England will starve. Our towns and cities will crumble, and trees will grow amongst the ruins using the bones of dead men as fertiliser. Do you see? They want nothing less than our complete annihilation, Samuel. Without man, the fox will rule.

SAMUEL. That's why the rabbits are helping us?

WILLIAM. Exactly. I hypothesise that when I investigate those woods, I will find further evidence of an infestation.

SAMUEL. You'll find rabbit holes. Loads of bloody rabbit holes. And you don't need to... interpret the symbols of what that means.

WILLIAM. On the contrary, I do.

SAMUEL. Rabbits. In those woods. That's all. And when I see a rabbit, I shoot it. So I'm damn sure they're not trying to help me any.

Pause.

I'll show you. The rabbit holes. Come on.

WILLIAM. No. Thank you.

Pause. SAMUEL *is at a loss.*

SAMUEL. Right. Well. You coming in for lunch? Judith'll have something laid out.

WILLIAM. No.

SAMUEL *nods, is about to leave.*

Samuel. While you're here, there's something I want to ask you.

SAMUEL. Oh?

WILLIAM. Your son. Daniel. How exactly did he die?

Pause.

I know this is hard for you, but the sons and daughters of farming families are a valuable shared resource for the future of this country. Daniel's death affects us all.

SAMUEL *looks as if he's considering punching* WILLIAM *in the face.* WILLIAM *takes a small step back. He puts on his gentlest tone of voice.*

Sam, I thought it better to spare Judith these questions. But if you'd prefer, I can ask her instead, this evening.

Pause.

SAMUEL. No. Ask me.

WILLIAM. How did Daniel die?

SAMUEL. Drowned.

WILLIAM. How?

· *Pause.*

SAMUEL. It was just getting dark. Jude had gone to Abe's to see Sarah. I put Dan to bed. Fell asleep in front of the fire. I woke up. I thought someone had said my name. But there was no one. I saw the door was open. I looked at the clock. My dad's clock. Ten past nine, exactly. I went upstairs. He wasn't there. I called for him. I went out... I looked everywhere.

Pause.

WILLIAM. Samuel?

SAMUEL. Found him. Found Dan. Dead… in two foot of flood water. He slipped in the mud, is what I reckon. He was all muddy.

Pause.

WILLIAM. Did you call for a doctor?

SAMUEL. I think he must of said my name. When he come downstairs. He said my name. Dad, he said. That's what I heard. In my sleep. But I didn't wake up quick enough.

WILLIAM. Did you call for a doctor?

SAMUEL. I should have locked the door. I should have… I was looking after him. It was my fault.

WILLIAM. Sam. Did you call a doctor?

SAMUEL. I tried to get him breathing. But he was dead. Cold.

WILLIAM. Then he must have been there for some time. If you woke because Daniel spoke to you, only a few minutes would have elapsed. He would still have been warm.

SAMUEL. It was a cold night.

WILLIAM. Hhm. A doctor came?

SAMUEL. Said he drowned.

WILLIAM. I'll have to see the death certificate.

SAMUEL *nods.*

SAMUEL. Ten past nine. I was going to give him that clock. My dad's clock.

Pause.

WILLIAM. Tell me… was Daniel a sleepwalker?

SAMUEL. No.

WILLIAM. He'd never gone outside by himself at night like this before?

SAMUEL. No.

WILLIAM. Thank you for telling me. I know that must have been hard.

Pause.

SAMUEL. I'm going in.

SAMUEL *leaves.* WILLIAM *makes a note in his notebook.*

6

JUDITH *is in the kitchen, setting the table.* WILLIAM *is watching her, and she is uncomfortable under his intense gaze.*

JUDITH. Did you, uh… have a good look round then?

WILLIAM. I did.

JUDITH *nods.*

JUDITH. The weather stayed clear for you.

WILLIAM. Yes.

Pause.

JUDITH. I wasn't sure if you'd be eating with us. You didn't come in for lunch.

WILLIAM. We try to avoid eating to excess.

JUDITH. No lunch?

WILLIAM. I had the bread you'd given me.

JUDITH. That's not enough. Not for breakfast and lunch together. Didn't you get hungry?

WILLIAM. Hunger is a suitable reminder of the spectre of starvation that haunts our land.

JUDITH. Oh. Why don't you sit down? Sam will be in soon.

WILLIAM. I will. Thank you.

WILLIAM *sits*.

Can I do anything to help?

JUDITH. No, no... you're our guest.

WILLIAM *is pleased to have been called a guest*.

WILLIAM. It does smell very... appetising.

JUDITH. You must be hungry. If you don't want to wait I can –

WILLIAM. No. I can wait.

Pause.

What is it?

JUDITH. Casserole.

WILLIAM. Oh, good.

Pause.

JUDITH. You must do a lot of travelling.

WILLIAM. So far, I've worked entirely in this county.

JUDITH. Like me then. I was born in the next village. Lived here all my life.

WILLIAM. It's a beautiful area. Very green. Very English.

JUDITH. Very wet.

WILLIAM. Indeed. Quintessentially English, in that respect.

JUDITH. Where are you from?

WILLIAM. Uh...

WILLIAM *frowns*.

I went to The Institute when I was five, to begin my training.

JUDITH. What about your parents?

WILLIAM. I'm sure they were very proud.

JUDITH *processes what* WILLIAM *has said. She's not quite sure what he means.*

JUDITH. Who looked after you… at The Institute?

WILLIAM. Each dormitory had a house father, and we were taught to consider this England… this… Earth… as the only mother we would ever need. Indeed, she is mother to us all.

JUDITH. Yes, but… she couldn't tell you a bedtime story. Or comfort you, when you felt afraid.

WILLIAM. She feeds us, she clothes us. She gives us everything we have. I think her a very good, kind mother.

JUDITH. And your… house father… was he kind?

Pause. WILLIAM *thinks.*

WILLIAM. He instilled in us the necessary discipline. I am often thankful to him for that.

JUDITH. Ah.

Pause.

WILLIAM. I was glad to leave him behind when I left The Institute to begin my work, but isn't every son glad to leave his father when he comes of age? My mother, though, will be with me always. When I want to see her, I go outside.

JUDITH. You never saw your real parents again?

WILLIAM. No.

JUDITH. I can't imagine giving up a child. Do you know why they –

WILLIAM. I walked up the hill today. And… the way the valley curves… it's like a mighty hand, cradling the farmhouse. As if the Earth sought to shelter those who live here.

JUDITH. Ah… it does. The worst of the wind breaks up on the ridge. The tops of the trees are bent, from growing into it. Did you see?

WILLIAM. No. It's a breathtaking view.

JUDITH. It puts things in perspective.

WILLIAM. Oh?

JUDITH. Our problems... our lives... they're so small. They don't matter. Not really. The sun rises every day... the wind blows, the rain falls. Things go on, just like they did... just like they did... before.

Pause.

WILLIAM. This year has been very hard for you.

JUDITH. Hard. Yes.

WILLIAM. Remember, the night is darkest just before the dawn. We suffer and toil to bring our country back into the light. History is watching us, Judith. We have to fight! We can't give up!

JUDITH. This farm is all we've got. I'd fertilise the fields with my own blood if I had to. I'll not give up.

WILLIAM *is impressed.*

WILLIAM. That's the spirit. But... I hope that you won't have to use such extreme measures.

JUDITH *smiles at* WILLIAM. *She puts a basket of bread down in front of him.*

JUDITH. Here. Help yourself.

WILLIAM *looks at the bread. He wants to take a piece, but instead he pushes it away from him and gets out his notebook. He opens it and readies himself for a moment before speaking.*

WILLIAM. Judith. Before Samuel gets back... I have a few more questions.

JUDITH. Oh?

WILLIAM. I need to ask about your... conjugal relations.

JUDITH *looks at* WILLIAM, *shocked.*

Nothing to worry about. Just a few easy questions.

JUDITH. Why do you want to ask me about that?

WILLIAM. I have to examine every part of my patient. Otherwise how can I be sure that I haven't left the tumour festering in the dark?

WILLIAM *tries a reassuring smile.* JUDITH *stares at him.*

I thought, given what you've said about Samuel's illness, that you'd prefer it if I put my questions to you. But I can put them to Samuel when –

JUDITH. No. I'll answer.

WILLIAM. Good. Could you sit down?

JUDITH *sits at the table.*

Judith. You and Samuel have no heir. This puts the long-term future of this farm in jeopardy.

JUDITH. We're trying for another baby.

WILLIAM. Ah. Good. That's good.

WILLIAM *makes a note.*

You are having regular… sexual intercourse?

JUDITH *nods.* WILLIAM *makes a note.*

With your husband?

JUDITH. What?

WILLIAM. I have to ask. Are you having intercourse with Samuel, or with other men?

JUDITH. With Sam!

WILLIAM. And is your husband having intercourse with anyone else? A neighbour, perhaps… Sarah?

JUDITH. No. Of course not. He's not… We're not like that!

WILLIAM *makes notes.*

WILLIAM. How many times a week do you have sexual intercourse? On average?

JUDITH. I don't know. Once. Twice.

WILLIAM. Have your sexual habits changed over the last year?

JUDITH. No.

WILLIAM. Does Samuel suggest new or unusual practices?

JUDITH. No.

WILLIAM. No violence or...

JUDITH. No!

WILLIAM. Good. Uh. In what position do you usually... uh.

WILLIAM *takes a breath. Swallows.*

Face to face? Or does he... uh... from behind...?

JUDITH. I don't see how that –

WILLIAM. Answer the question.

JUDITH. Face to face.

WILLIAM. Is it... good?

JUDITH. What?

WILLIAM. Is it good? Does he... does he make you orgasm?

JUDITH *stares at him.* WILLIAM *looks away, flushed.*

The door opens and SAMUEL *walks in.*

SAMUEL. More questions?

SAMUEL *glowers at* WILLIAM. WILLIAM *flips his notebook shut and puts it away.*

WILLIAM. Nothing important. I'm finished now.

SAMUEL. Finished? You're going then?

WILLIAM. I'm finished for today.

SAMUEL. Huh.

JUDITH. Dinner's nearly ready.

> JUDITH *gives* SAMUEL *a quick kiss on the cheek. He's not expecting it.*

Casserole. You like casserole.

SAMUEL. Aye. Aye.

> SAMUEL *takes off his coat and hangs it up. He washes his hands at the sink, and dries them with a clean tea towel.*

Temperature's dropping. Might be a frost tonight.

JUDITH. Good. It'll make the leeks sweet.

> SAMUEL *sits down at the table opposite* WILLIAM. *He takes some bread, butters it and tears off a chunk with his teeth. Chewing, he looks at* WILLIAM. WILLIAM *squirms a little under his gaze.*

SAMUEL. How old are you, Mr Bloor?

WILLIAM. I'm nineteen.

SAMUEL. 'S young.

WILLIAM. As I was telling Judith earlier… I began my training at the age of five.

SAMUEL. How many farms you been to then? How many…

JUDITH. Investigations.

SAMUEL. Aye.

WILLIAM. Three.

SAMUEL. Huh.

WILLIAM. I'm fully qualified, Samuel.

SAMUEL. Did they have foxes, those other farms?

JUDITH. That's none of our business. I'm sorry, William.

WILLIAM. I'm happy to say that my other investigations led me to conclude that the farms were simply victims of bad management and nothing more sinister.

SAMUEL. Bad farmers.

WILLIAM. Exactly.

JUDITH. What happened to them?

WILLIAM. I recommended that the farmers remain in residence and simply... try harder.

JUDITH *is heartened to hear this.*

JUDITH. You gave them a second chance.

WILLIAM. I did what I thought best for the productivity of the farms in question.

JUDITH *brings warm plates and a jug of water and puts them on the table.*

SAMUEL. He found a rabbit skull, Jude. Did he tell you?

JUDITH. No.

SAMUEL. It's a symbol, he says. A warning.

JUDITH. Oh?

WILLIAM. It could be. It's too early to say definitively.

SAMUEL. How long will it take to say?

WILLIAM. It's too early to say.

SAMUEL *glowers at* WILLIAM. *Annoyed,* WILLIAM *glares back.*

JUDITH *gets the casserole dish out of the oven and brings it to the table. She puts on a smile.*

JUDITH. Shall we eat?

7

WILLIAM *is sitting on the bed, his head in his hands.*

Anguished, he pulls off his nightshirt, reaches into his travelling bag and brings out a small whip.

He kneels on the floor and begins to whip himself, bringing the whip down rhythmically over his shoulders and onto his back.

WILLIAM. I. Am. Clean. In. Body. And. Mind.

8

The garden of SARAH'*s farmhouse.* SARAH *is pegging wet clothes – mostly children's clothes – on the line.* JUDITH *is helping her. Both keep one eye on their surroundings, looking out for anyone approaching.*

JUDITH. In the morning he takes some bread and he goes out. All day, even when it's raining. He comes back covered in mud... shivering, shaking... I feel sorry for him.

SARAH. I don't. I hope he catches pneumonia.

JUDITH. Sarah.

SARAH. What's he said? He going to give you the all-clear?

JUDITH. I don't know. He was friendly at first, to me at least. But now he's gone quiet. He has dinner with us every night and he barely speaks.

SARAH. Good. You won't have to listen to his idiocy.

JUDITH. A couple of times I've caught him looking at me...

SARAH. Looking at you how?

JUDITH. I'm not sure. It's strange.

SARAH. Well… he's been at yours a week today. Maybe that's how long they're supposed to stay. Maybe tomorrow morning he'll take his bread and his bags and bugger off.

Pause. JUDITH *doesn't look convinced.*

Abe says the worst thing we can do is panic. It'll make us look guilty. Arouse suspicion. We carry on as normal. All of us.

JUDITH. I can't be more normal without acting like a lunatic.

SARAH *smiles.*

SARAH. Did you read the pamphlet?

JUDITH. Yes.

SARAH. And?

JUDITH. Who wrote it? How do you know they're telling the truth?

SARAH. Have you ever seen a fox? Has anyone you know ever seen a fox?

JUDITH. Foxes are sly. Everyone knows that. Just because you can't see them. Doesn't mean they're not there.

SARAH. Wake up, Jude! It's a fairy story, the whole thing! The foxes are gone, but anyone who speaks out, anyone who talks about their doubts… they're arrested!

JUDITH. Why?

SARAH. Because they're terrified of the truth and what it can do, that's why! They don't know why the weather's gone bad, or the crops are failing, and they don't know how to stop it. They've been wrong all this time, and all those people who lost their farms… all those people who died… Something like this… It could bring the whole bloody Government down.

JUDITH. He believes it. William Bloor. He believes in what he's doing.

SARAH. Course he does. Wouldn't be very convincing otherwise, would he? Anyone will believe anything if you get to them young enough.

Pause. JUDITH *sighs.*

JUDITH. I don't know what to think. I just want him to give us the all-clear.

SARAH. He's not been over here yet. That's a good sign. And you said he's never found foxes before... Maybe he thinks you're behind because of... bad management.

JUDITH. Maybe.

SARAH. Abe was right. No point panicking. This could all come to nothing. So long as you keep on...

Rain begins to fall. SARAH *looks up.*

JUDITH. Being normal?

SARAH. Yes. Bloody hell.

The women unpeg the clothes from the line as quickly as they can.

One dry afternoon. That's all I needed....

They run off inside with the washing in their arms.

9

WILLIAM *stands in his room holding a large, leather-bound book.*

WILLIAM. The red fox, Vulpes Vulpes, is as the name suggests, most usually reddish brown, but its colour ranges to silver and black. It has slender paws, a long muzzle, erect, pointed ears and a tail covered in longer hairs, giving the appearance and name 'brush'. The eyes of the beast are a dull yellow-gold with dark, vertically oriented pupils like those of a cat.

Usually the size of a large dog, an adult male can grow up to two and a half metres long from nose to tail tip. Novices should be aware that from a distance, a large brown dog can resemble the beast, but their silhouettes are in fact quite different. Study the diagrams and illustrations that follow and submit them to memory to aid you in your identifications.

The fox is an omnivore and will eat almost anything; fruit, carrion, insects, and small- to medium-sized mammals such as mice and rabbits, unwary cats, small dogs, newborn lambs and sickly calves. Many incidences have been recorded of a mother leaving her baby unguarded outside for only a few seconds, returning to find it gone, taken and devoured. The beast's bloodlust far outstrips its appetite and it will slaughter every hen in a henhouse, leaving the headless carcasses behind. A perfectly evolved killing machine, the beast's teeth can grow up to ten centimetres in length, and its claws can disembowel a man. Sly in nature, the beast is active mainly at dusk and during the night, when it can go about its deadly work unseen.

The beast has influence over the weather, and blights farmers' crops with unseasonable rainfall or periods of drought. It can also cause fires (see 'Fox Fire', Chapter Four), and is riddled with parasites and dangerous diseases to which it is immune but which it revels in spreading about the countryside.

The fox has powers to confuse and can send visions to the mentally unstable and disturb the dreams of the weak. Under its influence, the good and hard-working become fat, lazy alcoholics or...

WILLIAM *is disturbed. He takes a minute to collect himself.*

Or sexual perverts.

Some are victims, turned away from their honest labours unwillingly. Others have allowed the beast to sway their minds or welcomed it with open arms. Differentiating between the guilty and the innocent is very difficult and it is better to view all those living on contaminated farms with suspicion.

You, foxfinder, must be clean in body and mind. Always remember that the smallest fault in your character could become a crack into which the beast may insinuate himself, like water awaiting the freeze that will smash the stone apart.

Clutching the book to his chest, WILLIAM *sits down on the bed.*

10

WILLIAM *is sitting at the kitchen table. It's almost dark. He looks nervous. He gets up. Looks out of the window. Paces. Sits back down again.*

JUDITH *and* SAMUEL *enter in coats and boots.* JUDITH *has mud all over her hands and front.*

WILLIAM. Judith. Samuel. Where have you been?

SAMUEL. Pigs got out.

JUDITH. We've been out there an hour trying to catch them. I went over in the mud like an idiot. Thank God the rain let up before –

WILLIAM. Are you injured?

JUDITH. No, no.

WILLIAM. Good. I'm glad you're back. I need to –

SAMUEL. Pigs are smart. If someone leaves their gate unlatched, they'll open it.

WILLIAM. I didn't leave the gate open.

SAMUEL. Huh.

JUDITH. I'm sorry, William. You must be starving. I haven't had a chance to put dinner on yet.

SAMUEL. Could have put it on himself if he was that hungry. Don't they teach you how to cook at your Institute?

WILLIAM. There's something we need to discuss.

JUDITH. Oh.

SAMUEL *lets out a weary sigh.*

SAMUEL. Can we take our coats off first?

WILLIAM. Yes. Yes, I suppose so.

SAMUEL *and* JUDITH *take off their coats.* JUDITH *wipes her hands clean.*

JUDITH. Should I put some coffee on?

WILLIAM. No. Sit down. Please.

They sit down at the table. WILLIAM *takes the fox leaflet that* SARAH *gave to* JUDITH *out of his pocket and puts it on the table in front of them. He smoothes it out.*

Would either of you like to explain this?

SAMUEL. What is it?

WILLIAM. Propaganda. This leaflet supports the fox and his kind.

JUDITH. Someone shoved that in my hand when I was at the market last week.

WILLIAM. Someone?

JUDITH. It could have been anyone. It was crowded. I meant to burn it. I'll burn it now.

JUDITH *tries to take the pamphlet but* WILLIAM *takes it and puts it back in his pocket.*

WILLIAM. I'll keep hold of that, thank you.

JUDITH. I couldn't throw it on the floor, could I? What if a child had picked it up… or someone saw it and thought I was the one giving them out?

WILLIAM. I found it in the pocket of your dress.

SAMUEL. You went through my wife's dresses?

WILLIAM. I searched the house and the outbuildings while you were both out today.

SAMUEL. You've no right!

WILLIAM. On the contrary. I have special dispensation to search the properties of anyone under my suspicion.

JUDITH. I forgot about it. I forgot it was there.

WILLIAM. You wore the dress last week. On the day Sarah Box came to see you. Didn't you notice it still in your pocket?

JUDITH. There's often bits of paper in my pockets. Lists... notes...

SAMUEL. She's busy, for God's sake.

WILLIAM. Did you read it?

JUDITH. Only enough to see what it was.

WILLIAM *nods*.

WILLIAM. I don't think you were distributing these leaflets, Judith. But mere possession of this is enough to get you in serious trouble. You should have destroyed it as soon as you were given it.

JUDITH. I'll do that. If it ever happens again.

Pause.

WILLIAM. There's something else. As you both know, I spent this week examining your land. Early on, I noted several ominous signs, which required further investigation.

JUDITH. What signs?

WILLIAM. And on the second night, I became aware that the beast was... attempting to influence me.

JUDITH. What do you mean?

WILLIAM. It is impossible to explain to the untrained. Rest assured, I resisted him, easily. This... incident, the signs I have mentioned and your answers to my questions have led me to conclude that this farm is indeed suffering from contamination.

JUDITH. No. God, no.

WILLIAM. I know this is very serious news for you both.

SAMUEL. Did you see a fox?

WILLIAM. I wanted to confirm or deny my fears with an actual sighting and searched for hours both during the day and –

JUDITH. You didn't find anything.

WILLIAM. No.

JUDITH. So it's all right. You were mistaken.

WILLIAM. I was not mistaken! It is hardly surprising that I could not find the beast after an incomplete search of only a few days. In any case, there is enough evidence to confirm my belief, not least the cluster of negative events that occurred here in March this year and, I think, marked the beginning of his assault.

JUDITH. But if you haven't seen one how can you –

WILLIAM. I believe that the beasts may be responsible for the death of your son.

Pause. SAMUEL *and* JUDITH *are speechless.*

Your son was not a sleepwalker. There was no reason for him to go outside. He had never done so before. Is that not correct?

JUDITH. He was curious. I think he woke up and went exploring.

WILLIAM. Curious. That fits my theory.

JUDITH. I don't...

WILLIAM. I suspect that the beasts were watching your house that night. They saw you, Judith, leave. They crept closer, and through the window saw you, Samuel, fall asleep. For a few moments Daniel lay unguarded and they used that time to call to him. They lured him outside. They led him into the muddy water and they laughed as he drowned.

JUDITH. It was an accident.

WILLIAM. There is cancer here, Judith. And if you ignore it, it will destroy you.

JUDITH. We don't have foxes.

WILLIAM. Continued denial of the infestation is one of the signs of collaboration. The corrupt farmer wants to hide the truth for as long as possible so that they can continue to sabotage their own farm and –

JUDITH. But we'd never!

WILLIAM. – hasten the collapse of civilisation. Is that what you want? To live wild and savage? To rut in the woods, grunting and sweating like a filthy beast?

JUDITH. No!

WILLIAM. Then you agree with my findings? Your farm is contaminated?

JUDITH. I... I suppose... it's possible.

WILLIAM *nods.*

WILLIAM. Good. Good.

JUDITH. What does this mean... for us?

WILLIAM. I will need to perform a more extensive examination before I can make any recommendations. It may take some time.

JUDITH *takes* WILLIAM*'s hand.*

JUDITH. I swear to you... we're not collaborators.

WILLIAM *is disturbed by her close proximity.*

WILLIAM. I, uh...

He draws his hand away from hers.

I have work to do. Could you make me a simple sandwich, and bring it to my room? Be sure to knock before you enter.

JUDITH *nods*. WILLIAM *goes upstairs*.

JUDITH. Oh God. What do we do now?

SAMUEL. Make him his sandwich. You sit down. I'll do it.

11

The fields.

WILLIAM *is standing in the darkness, notebook in hand.*

Suddenly SAMUEL *appears out of the dark. He is carrying a shotgun. He scares* WILLIAM.

WILLIAM. Samuel!

SAMUEL. Seen anything tonight?

WILLIAM. What are you doing out here?

SAMUEL. I need to see.

WILLIAM. See...?

SAMUEL. Two people looking. More likely to find what's there to be found.

WILLIAM. Absolutely not. No.

SAMUEL. It's my land. My responsibility.

WILLIAM. That's an admirable attitude, but you can't help me. My superiors would not accept your findings as the truth.

SAMUEL. They accept your word?

WILLIAM. They do.

SAMUEL. Then we stay together.

WILLIAM. No. I'm sorry.

Pause.

SAMUEL. Where've you looked so far?

WILLIAM. I am working to a grid system. I've walked the entire farm in daylight. And I am now working my way across the grid in darkness.

SAMUEL. You looked in the woods at night?

WILLIAM. No.

SAMUEL. Why not? If an animal's hiding, that's where it is.

WILLIAM. I'm working from the south.

SAMUEL. Wood's in the north.

WILLIAM. I know that.

SAMUEL. No point leaving it till last.

WILLIAM. I eliminate one square at a time.

SAMUEL. Huh. What d'you do if you see one?

WILLIAM. The beast can be deadly. We do not approach him. We retreat and make our report.

SAMUEL. Can't make a report if the deadly beast rips you groin to gullet. Can you?

WILLIAM. The beast is unlikely to attack a fully grown man.

SAMUEL. You'd think they'd want you fully grown then. Not half-starved.

WILLIAM. I am perfectly capable of looking after myself!

SAMUEL. I've got this.

He indicates the shotgun. Pause.

But you don't want my help.

Pause.

WILLIAM. Will you follow my methods and do as I say?

SAMUEL. I will.

WILLIAM. As I said. We eliminate one square at a time.

12

SAMUEL *and* JUDITH*'s bedroom, later that night.* JUDITH *is lying in the bed.* SAMUEL *enters. He's trying to be quiet, but* JUDITH *is already awake.*

JUDITH. Where've you been?

SAMUEL. I went out.

JUDITH. You can't just... in the middle of the night! I didn't know where you'd gone!

SAMUEL. I'm all right. I heard him go, so I followed. I'm helping him look.

JUDITH. What?

Pause.

SAMUEL. What he said makes sense. No reason for Dan to go out like that.

JUDITH. Dan went out because he was bored, or because he thought I was outside, or because –

SAMUEL. Because I didn't lock the door before I fell asleep.

Pause.

JUDITH. I was the one who went out and left the door unlocked! Why don't you try blaming me, instead of yourself?

Pause.

SAMUEL. Could be they did it.

JUDITH. No, Sam.

SAMUEL. I heard something that night. I thought it was Dan, but it could have been them.

JUDITH. No! For God's sake, we don't have foxes!

SAMUEL. He's going to hear you.

JUDITH. We don't have foxes! You know that. You said that to me a week ago.

SAMUEL. I've never looked properly. Another thing I should have done.

JUDITH. It wasn't your fault, it wasn't foxes, it was an accident!

SAMUEL. If they're out there, I'll find them. Then we'll know.

13

SARAH *and Abraham's farmhouse kitchen.*

WILLIAM *is sitting at the table. His notebook is in front of him. He is waiting.* SARAH *enters. She's shocked and horrified to see* WILLIAM.

SARAH. Mr Bloor?

WILLIAM. Good afternoon, Sarah. How are you?

SARAH. I'm... fine. Thank you.

WILLIAM. There was no one here so I decided to come in.

SARAH. The door was locked.

WILLIAM. Yes. You don't mind, do you?

SARAH. No, not at all! No point standing outside in the rain. How long have you been waiting?

WILLIAM. Not long.

SARAH. If I'd known you were coming... I'll get you a cup of tea. And I've got some –

WILLIAM. No, thank you. Why don't you sit down?

SARAH *sits.*

I've taken a look at your numbers. In terms of productivity, you have been slightly behind this year. However, with a good winter harvest, you will make your quota.

SARAH. Yes.

WILLIAM. I walked your land today. You are suffering from significant flooding in low-lying areas.

SARAH. It'll dry out, in the spring.

WILLIAM. Perhaps, but from my observations today I'd hypothesise that your winter harvest has been ruined. You won't make your quota.

SARAH. There's still time. We're hoping for the best.

WILLIAM *makes a note*.

WILLIAM. Nathanial and Rebecca. How are they?

SARAH. Happy. Healthy.

WILLIAM. Excellent. And your husband. Abraham... he's fifty this year. Is that right?

SARAH. Fifty. Yes.

WILLIAM. That's quite an age gap.

SARAH. You can't help who you fall in love with.

WILLIAM. How is his health?

SARAH. He's an ox.

WILLIAM. An ox with a weak chest.

SARAH. No...

WILLIAM. I have a doctor's report here. Bronchitis.

SARAH. That was years ago! And it's not come back.

WILLIAM. Abraham was hospitalised.

SARAH. Only for a few days.

WILLIAM. A week.

SARAH. He's healthy now. I'll go and get him. He can tell you about it himself.

WILLIAM. That won't be necessary. You have a wonderful family.

SARAH. I do.

WILLIAM. Many people would view your life here as one of almost unimaginable good fortune.

SARAH. I know that.

WILLIAM. You have access to fresh vegetables, meat, eggs, dairy products...

SARAH. Yes.

WILLIAM. City dwellers have one egg a week on their ration, and three ounces of cheese. A factory worker... well... they live on what they get. A factory worker would think you very, very lucky.

SARAH shifts uncomfortably in her chair. She's not sure what WILLIAM is getting at.

A man like your husband. A strong man with a weak chest... how long do you think he'd last in the factories?

SARAH. I don't know.

WILLIAM. The current life expectancy is three years. How long do you think Abraham would last?

SARAH. I don't know.

WILLIAM. Guess.

SARAH. Three. Three years.

WILLIAM. If we took your farm, and sent you and your husband to work in the factories, you'd never see your children again.

Pause. SARAH is frozen with fear.

They would go to an orphanage. Perhaps Rebecca would be adopted. She's the younger... isn't she? Would you like your children to be raised by strangers?

Pause.

I have something to show you.

WILLIAM *takes the fox leaflet out of his pocket. He puts it on the table.*

Pause.

I found this at Judith's house. In the pocket of the dress she was wearing when she saw you last week. You gave it to her. Didn't you?

SARAH. No.

WILLIAM. I had hours to search your house before you came back. I found a stack of these leaflets, hidden under a floorboard.

Pause.

SARAH. They're not mine. I'm keeping them safe for someone.

WILLIAM. Who?

Pause.

You gave this… poison to Judith. Didn't you?

SARAH. People need to know the truth.

WILLIAM. Oh yes. Very clever. Convince England that her enemy is defeated. And when we lower our defences… you and your kind rise up and destroy us all! Who gave you the leaflets?

Pause.

If you force me to report your farm as the source of this propaganda, you and Abe will swiftly find yourselves working in the factories.

SARAH. Abe doesn't know about it! I only gave one to Jude… no one else.

WILLIAM. Then protect yourself. Tell me who made the leaflets.

SARAH. I'll tell you if you give me your word as a foxfinder that you'll keep me and mine out of it.

WILLIAM. Are you trying to bribe me?

SARAH. I'm trying to make a trade.

WILLIAM. A foxfinder can't be bought. If you won't tell me, we have nothing more to say to each other.

WILLIAM *gets up to leave.*

SARAH. I'll give you the name, and something else. Information.

WILLIAM. I said I can't be bought.

SARAH. It's about Jude and Sam. Two things.

Pause. SARAH *has got* WILLIAM's *interest. He frowns.*

WILLIAM. I thought you and Judith were friends.

SARAH. We are.

WILLIAM. And yet you'd betray her?

SARAH. Do you want to know, or not?

WILLIAM *thinks.*

WILLIAM. Yes.

SARAH. Give me your word.

WILLIAM. You have my word. I'll keep you and Abraham out of my report.

SARAH. James Cross. The baker. He's the one.

WILLIAM *makes a note of this.*

WILLIAM. And the information?

SARAH. Did you know Sam was ill?

WILLIAM. I did. Judith told me it was the flu.

SARAH. She lied.

WILLIAM. I already knew that. It was obvious.

SARAH. But do you know what was really wrong with him?

WILLIAM. Go on.

SARAH. When Dan died in March, Sam got into bed. And he didn't get out until June.

WILLIAM. He was ill?

SARAH. He just lay there. Barely ate, barely spoke. Jude had to take charge of everything, and she was grieving too. That's why they're so behind.

WILLIAM. I see.

WILLIAM *makes a note.*

And the second piece of information? Sarah? If you won't tell me I'll have to cancel our trade.

SARAH. Jude told you they're trying for another baby.

WILLIAM. Yes?

SARAH. But they're not. They haven't had sex since Dan died.

WILLIAM *is shocked.*

WILLIAM. This is a decision they've made?

SARAH. No. Jude wants to. But Sam... he can't.

WILLIAM. Do you mean that he's physically incapable?

SARAH. They haven't tried. He won't. That's what I mean.

Pause.

It's not Jude's fault. And Sam's better. They'll get back on their feet in no time. They're good farmers. You're not going to take their farm, are you?

WILLIAM. I think it's a little late for you to worry about that. Goodnight, Sarah.

WILLIAM *gets up and takes his coat.*

SARAH. Can I ask you a question?

WILLIAM. What is it?

SARAH. Have you ever seen a fox?

WILLIAM. Not yet.

SARAH. Has anyone you know ever seen a fox?

WILLIAM. Of course.

SARAH. Who?

WILLIAM. My teachers at The Institute told me countless stories of coming face to face with the beast.

SARAH. Stories. Old stories.

WILLIAM. Not so old.

SARAH. What about the young foxfinders, the ones like you?

WILLIAM. In the past six months alone, my colleagues have discovered several contaminated properties.

SARAH. But did they see any foxes?

WILLIAM. No.

SARAH. Don't you think that's… incredible?

WILLIAM. The fox is sly. Everyone knows that.

SARAH. They tell us that to explain why we never see one.

WILLIAM. I know what you're trying to do, but –

SARAH. We never see one because they're all gone, and killing them didn't make things better, because they were never our enemy!

WILLIAM. You might as well save your breath. Your filthy propaganda will have no effect on me.

SARAH. They taught you to believe in a pack of lies, and they're using you to keep the rest of us believing. You've been played for a bloody fool, can't you see that?

WILLIAM. I see nothing but a diseased collaborator.

SARAH. We have to find the real reasons for our problems, or things'll just go on, getting worse and worse!

WILLIAM. Our trade is cancelled. Peddle this misinformation in the factories, if you can.

SARAH. You gave your word as a foxfinder that you'd keep me and mine safe.

WILLIAM. You just tried to convince me that my mission, and therefore my word, is meaningless.

SARAH. If you break it, I'll know I'm right.

Seething with rage, WILLIAM *turns to leave.*

WILLIAM. Stay away from Judith and Samuel.

SARAH. Will you keep your word to me? Mr Bloor?

WILLIAM *has gone. The door slams shut behind him.* SARAH *blows out a long breath.*

14

WILLIAM'*s bedroom, later that night.*

WILLIAM *is in bed, restless.*

After a moment he throws himself out of the bed, pulls off his nightshirt and reaches under the bed for his bag. He brings out the whip.

He brings it down on his back. Almost instantaneously, someone bangs on the door. WILLIAM *jumps.*

SAMUEL (*off*). William!

WILLIAM. Wait! Don't come in.

WILLIAM'*s barely had time to push the whip back into his travelling bag before* SAMUEL *opens the door. He strides straight over to the window and looks outside.* WILLIAM *frantically pulls a shirt on.*

What in God's name –

SAMUEL. Did you hear it?

WILLIAM. What?

SAMUEL. A fox. I heard a fox!

WILLIAM. When?

SAMUEL. Just now! You must of heard it.

> JUDITH *comes into the room. She's wearing her nightgown.*
> WILLIAM *pulls his trousers on.*

JUDITH. What is it? What happened?

WILLIAM. Samuel heard a fox.

SAMUEL. Did you hear it?

JUDITH. I heard you shouting, that's all.

SAMUEL. She was asleep. I'm going down. Might still catch it.

WILLIAM. Hold on, hold on.

> WILLIAM *opens the leather-bound book.*

JUDITH. What did you hear, Sam?

SAMUEL. A fox! A bloody fox!

JUDITH. Yes, but –

WILLIAM. Fox call. Here it is… dog-like barks and yelps… and the fox mating cry, a sound not unlike a human screaming.

SAMUEL. Aye. The scream. That's it. Didn't you hear it?

WILLIAM. No.

JUDITH. Nor did I.

SAMUEL. You were both asleep, then.

WILLIAM. I was… awake. But this room and your room are on opposite sides of the house. It must have been outside your room calling up. That's why I didn't hear anything.

SAMUEL. Aye, that'll be it.

WILLIAM. Incredible. This is proof, Samuel. Proof!

SAMUEL. I'm going to look.

WILLIAM. We can't go rushing off unprepared.

SAMUEL. Aye. Could be a trap. I'll take the gun.

WILLIAM. That's not what I meant. We should stay calm, stick to the grid and continue our search as planned tomorrow night.

SAMUEL. Huh. I'll look in the garden. There might be prints.

WILLIAM. Oh, yes, I'll come with you, just let me put my...

SAMUEL *goes out.*

Samuel! Wait!

WILLIAM *pulls on his boots.*

JUDITH. William...

WILLIAM. Excuse me.

WILLIAM *rushes out.*

15

JUDITH *and* SAMUEL*'s farmhouse kitchen. Half an hour later.*

JUDITH *is in the kitchen.* SAMUEL *and* WILLIAM *enter from outside.* WILLIAM *looks disappointed.*

JUDITH. Did you find any prints?

WILLIAM. No.

JUDITH. Nothing?

SAMUEL. Just means he's too smart to walk in the mud.

JUDITH. The whole garden's muddy. How could a fox get underneath our window to call up without leaving prints?

WILLIAM. Uh...

JUDITH. Sam, maybe you were dreaming.

SAMUEL. I heard it, I tell you!

JUDITH. It could have been a rabbit caught in a snare. Or an owl.

SAMUEL. I know what an owl sounds like! He believes me, don't you?

Pause.

WILLIAM. Yes. Tomorrow we'll redouble our efforts. I feel certain that we will find something.

SAMUEL. Aye. I'm going to bed.

SAMUEL *walks off upstairs.* JUDITH *looks at* WILLIAM.

JUDITH. I didn't hear a scream, and I'm a light sleeper. You didn't hear it, and you were awake.

WILLIAM. As I said, the rooms are on opposite sides of the house.

JUDITH. A scream would have carried through.

WILLIAM. Not necessarily.

JUDITH. I think Sam might have... imagined it.

Pause. WILLIAM *thinks.*

WILLIAM. The fox can manipulate people's dreams. Did you know that?

JUDITH. No.

WILLIAM. Perhaps he called to Samuel in his dream. That would explain why neither of us heard it and why there are no prints outside the house.

JUDITH. I'm sure you know what you're talking about, but... Sam didn't even know what a fox call sounded like until you read that description out of your book.

Pause. WILLIAM *looks at* JUDITH, *doubt on his face.*

WILLIAM. That's not important.

JUDITH. Right. Well, goodnight then.

WILLIAM. Yes. Goodnight.

> JUDITH *goes upstairs.* WILLIAM *sinks down into a chair, frowning.*

16

JUDITH *and* SAMUEL'*s farmhouse kitchen, very early morning.* JUDITH *is talking to a nervous* SARAH.

SARAH. He's not here?

JUDITH. No.

SARAH. Where is he?

JUDITH. He went out with Sam last night and they're not back yet.

SARAH. Are you sure?

JUDITH. William! William!

> SARAH *cringes, but there is no response to* JUDITH'*s call.*

I went to your house to see you. Three times. Nobody came to the door.

SARAH. Oh.

JUDITH. I could hear you talking inside, but when I knocked you went quiet.

SARAH. It was a bad time.

JUDITH. It's all right. I understand. I'm dangerous. I've got the plague and you don't want to catch it. If I was you I wouldn't open the door to me either!

SARAH. What plague?

JUDITH. William says our farm's contaminated. I thought you'd heard. I thought that was why you...

SARAH. No. Something's happened.

JUDITH. What? What is it?

SARAH. We're leaving –

JUDITH. No.

SARAH. – and we want you to come with us.

Pause.

The foxfinder came to our house. He knew I gave you that leaflet.

JUDITH. I didn't tell him it was you.

SARAH. Didn't matter. He got in and searched the place, found some more there that I'd hidden. He was going to send me and Abe to the factories and put Nate and Becky in an orphanage! So I made a deal with him. I gave up the one who made the leaflets. James Cross. He's gone. The bakery's all closed up.

JUDITH. When was this?

SARAH. Wednesday.

JUDITH. It worked then. He didn't have you arrested. You don't need to leave. You're safe.

SARAH. No. That's the worst of it. Every night I lie awake thinking; tomorrow he'll change his mind. Tomorrow that bastard will decide it's his duty to turn us in.

JUDITH. You don't know that.

SARAH. Yes I do! Our lives are in his hands! We're not going to sit waiting for the blade to fall on our necks! We're getting out. Now. All of us.

Pause. JUDITH *is upset.*

JUDITH. Where?

SARAH. Some old friends have got a big place in Scotland. It's a dump, but it'll do. We'll go there, ask if we can work. In return they'll hide us.

JUDITH. For the rest of your lives?

SARAH. Or until things change. It can't be too long. They can't hide the truth for ever...

JUDITH. You want to travel... without being caught... all the way to Scotland?

SARAH. We'll go by night. Sleep in the day.

JUDITH. What if you get there and your friends say no, they can't take the risk?

SARAH. Ha! Would you turn away free labour?

JUDITH. Don't make jokes!

SARAH. I'm not, they need the help! And they're good people.

JUDITH. They'd need to be bloody saints! If they say no –

SARAH. They won't!

JUDITH. You'll have no shelter, no food. You'll starve to death.

SARAH. I know other folk we can try if Scotland doesn't work. It's a good plan! Now go pack bags for you and Sam. We're leaving at seven.

JUDITH. Today?

SARAH. Yes! We're travelling light, mind; your warmest clothes, money, valuables, food and –

JUDITH. It's impossible.

SARAH. It's an adventure. That's what Abe's told the children.

JUDITH. Sam would never leave the farm.

SARAH. Talk to him. Make him!

JUDITH. William says that the foxes killed Dan. That it wasn't just an accident.

SARAH. Oh God.

JUDITH. Sam says he has to know if it's true. He's helping
William! They've been out there every night this week,
looking.

SARAH. He believes it?

JUDITH. He wanted to. Now he does. He's started hearing
things, Sarah… and the way he talks… it's scaring me to
death.

Pause.

SARAH. You'll have to leave him behind.

JUDITH. I can't do that!

SARAH. He's no husband to you.

JUDITH. He's the only one I wanted.

SARAH. See sense, Jude!

JUDITH. I won't run while there's still a chance.

SARAH. Of what? Dying in the factories? No. No, you're
coming with us. Get your things and meet us by the bridge at
seven. We won't be able to wait long… Don't be late and
don't let either of them know what you're doing. You'll
come, won't you?

JUDITH *nods.*

JUDITH. You're a good friend to me.

They hug briefly.

SARAH. Seven o'clock.

SARAH *leaves.*

JUDITH *watches her go.*

17

The fields.

Early morning. SAMUEL *is standing with the shotgun hanging in one hand.* WILLIAM *has sunk into a miserable crouch and is almost asleep. They have been here for most of the night.* WILLIAM *rouses himself.*

WILLIAM. It's time to go in.

SAMUEL *doesn't move.* WILLIAM *sighs.*

The fox is abroad in the evening and during the night. It's getting light. We won't see anything now.

SAMUEL. Sssh.

Pause.

WILLIAM. Samuel, I admire your… tenacity. But even the strictest of my teachers at The Institute would tell me to make sure I get enough rest. We must go back to the farmhouse and refresh ourselves for tomorrow's… I mean tonight's… assault.

SAMUEL. Huh.

Pause.

WILLIAM. We can cross this square off. We've been here long enough. Let's go in.

SAMUEL. You go.

WILLIAM. I can't leave you in the field alone. You know that.

SAMUEL. Stay then.

WILLIAM *sinks back towards the ground. A long pause.*

WILLIAM. I've never actually seen a fox. Do you think that's... strange?

SAMUEL. No.

WILLIAM. One of my colleagues, Mr Jacob Fairweather, discovered a cluster of contaminated farms. Five farms... and yet he didn't see a single fox.

SAMUEL. Foxes are sly.

WILLIAM. Yes. Jacob could see the evidence, the signs of his influence, but the beast himself was too clever, too canny, too... sly, to be seen. If in that case he did not see the beast... then it's no wonder that I... or even you... or any of my colleagues... it's no wonder that we've never seen one. Is it?

SAMUEL. Shhh.

WILLIAM *frowns. A long pause.*

WILLIAM. We've yet to find so much as a single paw print on your farm. There are no prints, no sign of a den or hiding place, no droppings... But you could say that the absence of the fox is another sign of his presence and is to be expected.

SAMUEL. He's here. I know it.

WILLIAM. Yes. Of course he is.

Pause.

SAMUEL. You see that?

WILLIAM. What?

SAMUEL. On the fence. Just there.

SAMUEL *points to a nearby fence.*

WILLIAM. What? What am I looking at?

SAMUEL. Those white things, like flags.

WILLIAM. Uh...

SAMUEL. Tha's sheep's wool. Caught on the wire.

WILLIAM. There aren't any sheep on your farm.

SAMUEL. Abraham Box used this field to graze his flock a few months back, when his was too wet. Look. There's a pattern.

WILLIAM. Is there?

SAMUEL. Dot, dot, dot. Dash, dash, dash. Dot, dot, dot. Tha's Morse code. S – O – S. It's a sign. A warning.

WILLIAM *peers at the fence.*

WILLIAM. No, Samuel. That's just... wool.

SAMUEL. That rabbit skull you found. That looked just like a skull. But it wasn't. It was a sign. That's what you said.

WILLIAM. Uh. Yes.

SAMUEL. I'm telling you. That right there, that's a sign.

Confused, WILLIAM *looks again.*

WILLIAM. Ah, yes. I think I see the pattern now. You're right.

SAMUEL. Follow that fence, you get to the woods. The sheep are telling us, that's where they are. And that's where we'll go, tonight.

WILLIAM. No, we still have another three squares of the grid to search before we get to that area.

SAMUEL. You won't come, I'll go alone.

WILLIAM. You know I can't allow that! What if you saw something and I wasn't there to verify it?

SAMUEL. It's your job to find the fox. If you won't do it, I'll do it for you.

WILLIAM *sighs, defeated.*

WILLIAM. All right. If we... if I, search the rest of the grid afterwards, we can go to the woods tonight. Now... can we please go in?

SAMUEL. Aye. Aye.

SAMUEL *strides off, and* WILLIAM *follows.*

18

JUDITH *and* SAMUEL*'s farmhouse kitchen.*

JUDITH *is sitting at the table, a cup of coffee in her hand. She's been here since* SARAH *left.* WILLIAM *and* SAMUEL *enter from outside.* WILLIAM *is exhausted.*

SAMUEL. Jude.

WILLIAM. Good morning, Judith.

JUDITH. What time is it?

SAMUEL. Nine.

> JUDITH *nods.* WILLIAM *sits down at the table.*

WILLIAM. Is there anything to eat?

> JUDITH *pushes the bread basket over to him.*

JUDITH. It's stale.

WILLIAM. Oh.

JUDITH. I didn't have time yesterday to make any fresh. I've had to do all of Sam's work too... as he's been so busy helping you.

WILLIAM. I didn't ask for, nor do I need, Samuel's help.

JUDITH. The leeks need bringing in, Sam. Soon, or they'll rot.

SAMUEL. Won't be much longer. We're making progress.

JUDITH. You found something?

WILLIAM. No.

SAMUEL. Yes. We found a sign. Telling us where to look.

JUDITH. A sign.

SAMUEL. We'll go to the woods tonight.

WILLIAM. Excuse me. I'm going to get some rest. Samuel, I suggest that you do the same.

WILLIAM *gets up and stumbles out.*

JUDITH *pours coffee for* SAMUEL. *She lowers her voice.*

JUDITH. Sarah and Abraham are gone.

SAMUEL. Gone?

JUDITH. Run away, with the children.

SAMUEL. Huh.

JUDITH. Is that all you can say? Our oldest friends!

SAMUEL. Must have had something to hide, if they've run.

JUDITH. They were afraid, Sam. I'm afraid.

SAMUEL. Nothing for you to be scared of.

JUDITH. Sarah asked me to go too. She said I should leave you behind.

Pause.

But I said no, because I love you.

SAMUEL. Aye.

SAMUEL *kisses* JUDITH *on the forehead. He gulps his coffee down and starts stuffing bread into his pockets.*

JUDITH. What are you doing?

SAMUEL. I've to go back out. Need some things.

JUDITH. Things? What things?

SAMUEL. For tonight. I'm going to find them, and I'm going to kill them. The ones who killed our son.

JUDITH. It was an accident!

SAMUEL. I'd like to use dogs. More painful. But a bullet will do it. I'll bring back the heads, so you can spit on them.

JUDITH. Don't go back out there.

SAMUEL. It's you I'm doing this for.

JUDITH. No it's not!

Furious, JUDITH *slams her hands down on the table.*

I want you to forget about foxes and stay with me tonight!
Please, Sam. I need you to be strong now.

SAMUEL. When the foxes are gone, things'll get better. Us.
The farm. The future. Like you said. Wish me good hunting.

JUDITH *turns away.*

SAMUEL *leaves.* JUDITH *starts to cry.*

19

WILLIAM's *bedroom, later.*

WILLIAM *is lying on the bed in his shirt and trousers, asleep.*

There's a gentle knock at the door. Then another, but WILLIAM
doesn't wake up.

Slowly, JUDITH *pushes the door open.*

JUDITH. William?

WILLIAM. Hhh?

JUDITH. William.

WILLIAM. Judith… what?

JUDITH. I know you're tired, but…

WILLIAM. Uh. Come in.

JUDITH *sits down on the bed.* WILLIAM *is immediately on
edge.*

What… uh… what is it?

JUDITH. I need to ask you something.

WILLIAM. Of course.

JUDITH. Whatever you find out there tonight, you have to leave tomorrow. Please.

WILLIAM. I'm sorry?

JUDITH. I'm asking you to leave tomorrow.

WILLIAM. But my investigation isn't complete.

JUDITH. You say we've got foxes, we agree. Surely that's all you need?

WILLIAM. I'm afraid not. I have to finish my searches before I make my report.

JUDITH. Say you finished. I'll swear that you did if they come asking.

WILLIAM. A foxfinder doesn't lie.

JUDITH. What difference does it make? If you're going to report that we're contaminated, can't you just do it and leave?

WILLIAM. I have to complete my investigation.

JUDITH takes WILLIAM's hands in her own.

JUDITH. Please. You have to go, I'm begging you. Please.

WILLIAM. I'm sorry, Judith –

JUDITH. You say you want to help us, but all you've done since you got here is make things worse!

WILLIAM. I've done all I can! I've ignored things you've said and done, ignored certain pieces of information... I know... for example... that Samuel was unfit to work the farm for several months after your son died.

JUDITH is shocked, but she tries to remain composed.

JUDITH. He was ill. I told you that.

WILLIAM. You lied. He didn't have the flu. Sarah Box told me the truth.

Pause. JUDITH digests this information.

JUDITH. Sam was better before you came, and he'll be fine again once you're gone. All this is upsetting him. That's why I want you to go.

WILLIAM. I've bent the rules for you already, more than I should have.

JUDITH. I didn't realise.

WILLIAM. Another foxfinder would have condemned you. Perhaps I should do so... But I... I think you deserve a second chance.

JUDITH. You do?

WILLIAM. I intend to state in my report that you are innocent of collaboration and should keep your farm.

JUDITH. Oh, thank you. Thank you.

JUDITH *hugs* WILLIAM *briefly. Overwhelmed, he closes his eyes before she lets him go, leaving him dizzy.*

You must be starving. Come down... I'll make you some breakfast.

JUDITH *goes out.*

WILLIAM. My God, my God.

20

The woods. Evening.

SAMUEL *is standing under a tree. He's tied a few long pieces of cord to its lower branches, and they are hanging down, fluttering in the breeze. He's holding a sack in one hand, and his shotgun is propped up against the tree trunk.*

SAMUEL *reaches into the bag and takes out a dead rabbit. He ties the rabbit to one of the cords so it's hanging in the air. He does this again, with another rabbit.*

WILLIAM *appears. He's out of breath.*

WILLIAM. Samuel.

SAMUEL. Catch.

> SAMUEL *throws a dead rabbit at* WILLIAM. *He catches it, then recoils in horror and drops it when he realises what it is. The rabbit leaves blood on his hands.*

> 'S just a rabbit. Tie it up, over there.

> SAMUEL *gestures to the tree.* WILLIAM *wipes his hands on his trousers and shakes his head. Sighing,* SAMUEL *picks up the rabbit himself and ties it to the tree.*

> They're on our side, you said. Huh. Sorry, rabbit.

WILLIAM. What is this? What are you doing?

SAMUEL. Baiting a trap.

> SAMUEL *ties another rabbit.*

> A hungry beast can't ignore the call of blood. Tha's his nature. He'll come, and I'll be waiting.

WILLIAM. This is completely against protocol.

SAMUEL. Don't tell anyone about it then.

WILLIAM. We're not supposed to approach the beast. We're supposed to observe, and make our report. There's an extermination team, specialised in –

SAMUEL. Don't need a team. I'll do it.

WILLIAM. The extermination team is better –

SAMUEL. God's sake! All you do is yap! Shut up!

> *There are now several rabbits hanging from the tree.* SAMUEL *throws another couple on the ground underneath the branches.*

> You should go in. It's not a job for a boy.

WILLIAM. I'm staying.

SAMUEL. Then stay by me. And keep quiet.

SAMUEL picks up his gun and the empty sack, and moves away from the tree. He takes up a position some distance away and settles down, with a good view of the tree. Unhappily, WILLIAM *joins him.*

Time passes. It gets darker. The wind picks up, rustling the tree branches.

SAMUEL *comes to attention. He talks in hushed tones.*

Smell that?

WILLIAM. What?

SAMUEL. Rotting meat. Piss.

WILLIAM. No.

SAMUEL. He's coming.

SAMUEL sees something. He aims the shotgun towards the tree.

There.

WILLIAM. Where?

SAMUEL. Going for the rabbit. But he can't get it. See his eyes?

WILLIAM. No. Where?

SAMUEL. Right in front of you!

WILLIAM. I don't...

SAMUEL. Mouth's hanging open. He's laughing. Bastard! There's another.

SAMUEL tracks the gun in a wide circle.

One there. One there. Circling us.

WILLIAM. I don't see anything.

SAMUEL. Bastards. Bastards.

SAMUEL raises the gun and fires.

There's another. Three of them.

WILLIAM. There's nothing there.

SAMUEL. Killed my son. Made me sick. I'll kill you!

SAMUEL *fires again.*

'S not like a normal beast. Not scared. The way it looks...
like it knows you...

WILLIAM *grabs hold of* SAMUEL *and shakes him.*

WILLIAM. There's nothing there. No foxes. Nothing! Put the
gun down!

SAMUEL. Get off me.

SAMUEL *easily throws* WILLIAM *off. He falls.* SAMUEL
starts reloading the gun.

Running. Like cowards! I'll catch you...

SAMUEL *runs out after the foxes, leaving* WILLIAM
standing by the tree.

WILLIAM. There's nothing out there.

WILLIAM *sinks down to the ground and begins to sob.
From somewhere in the distance comes the sound of the
shotgun. Then another shot, further away.*

*A long pause, silent but for the wind in the leaves and
WILLIAM's sobbing. Then a loud crack comes from nearby
as someone steps on a twig.* WILLIAM *gasps with fear.*

Who's that? Who's there?

JUDITH *appears from between the trees, carrying a paraffin
lantern.*

JUDITH. Oh my God, William?

Concerned, JUDITH *puts the lantern down and goes over to*
WILLIAM.

William? Are you hurt?

WILLIAM. No.

JUDITH. What happened?

WILLIAM. You shouldn't be out here.

JUDITH. Neither should Sam. I'm taking him in. Where is he? I heard shots!

WILLIAM. He ran off.

JUDITH. Where to?

WILLIAM. He's shooting foxes.

JUDITH *is horrified to hear this.*

JUDITH. He's what?

WILLIAM. He sees them but I can't. Why can't I see them?

JUDITH. I don't know.

WILLIAM. If you went after him, would you see them?

JUDITH. I...

Pause.

WILLIAM. Would you?

JUDITH. I don't know.

WILLIAM. Do you believe that there are foxes on this farm?

JUDITH. Yes.

WILLIAM. You have to say that. I told you denial was a sign of collaboration.

Pause.

It's all lies. Isn't it?

Not sure what to say, JUDITH *doesn't speak. Her lack of response is all the answer* WILLIAM *needs.*

Does everyone know?

JUDITH. I don't know. I don't think so.

WILLIAM. Oh God. They told me my doubts were a sign of weakness...

Desperately, he clutches at JUDITH.

My mission. My life…

JUDITH. It's all right.

WILLIAM. Oh God… please…

He sobs. JUDITH *comforts him.*

JUDITH. Ssh. It's all right. It's all right. Ssh.

WILLIAM *kisses* JUDITH. *She pulls away, shocked.*

William… no. I'm sorry. I don't…

WILLIAM. I thought you… You were kind to me.

JUDITH. Kind, and that's all. I'm married.

Pause.

WILLIAM. He hasn't touched you in months. Sarah Box told me.

JUDITH. That's got nothing to do with it! I'm going to find Sam.

WILLIAM. No, you can't. He's shooting into the trees. It's too dangerous.

WILLIAM *moves in front of her, blocking her way.*

JUDITH. Sam would never hurt me.

WILLIAM. Stay here. Please. I…

WILLIAM *tries to kiss her again. She pushes him off.*

JUDITH. I said no.

WILLIAM. All my life I've denied myself the things I wanted. That's what a foxfinder does, for the sake of his mission.

JUDITH. Let me past, please. I need to find Sam.

WILLIAM. I've dreamed of you day and night for fifteen days. It's been like torture!

JUDITH. That's not my fault.

WILLIAM. Judith…

JUDITH. Get out of my way.

Pause. WILLIAM *becomes very calm.*

WILLIAM. I'll make a trade with you.

JUDITH. What?

WILLIAM. I'll go. I'll leave tomorrow, and I'll give your farm the all clear. If you… sleep with me.

Pause.

JUDITH. No.

WILLIAM. Then… I'll say the foxes came here because of you, because you're a drunk, an adulterer. I'll say you have sex with animals, that you're the foxes' whore.

JUDITH. You wouldn't.

Pause. He looks at her.

I thought you were better than this.

WILLIAM. I thought I was a lot of things.

Slowly, JUDITH *lies down on the ground.*

WILLIAM *gets on top of her and awkwardly begins to have sex with her. She turns her face away from him.*

SAMUEL *appears out of the dark. He stands there, his eyes wild. He has the shotgun.*

SAMUEL. You!

JUDITH. Sam!

WILLIAM *gets up. He backs away from* SAMUEL, *who advances upon him.*

WILLIAM. Please… please don't.

SAMUEL *shoots* WILLIAM *in the chest. He falls.* JUDITH *looks at* SAMUEL *in horror.*

SAMUEL. I shot a fox.

22

JUDITH *and* SAMUEL*'s farmhouse kitchen. Two days later.*
JUDITH *and* SAMUEL *are sitting in their Sunday best. Winter sunshine is pouring in through the windows.* JUDITH *is extremely anxious, but* SAMUEL *is relaxed.*

JUDITH. What time is it?

SAMUEL. Quarter past.

JUDITH. I thought they'd be here by now.

SAMUEL. They'll be here soon.

Pause.

You were right about the leeks. Another few days in the field, they'd have been rotting.

Pause.

A good crop. Things're turning for the better already.

JUDITH *goes to the window and looks out.*

JUDITH. Where are they? I can't stand this waiting.

SAMUEL. They'll be here soon.

JUDITH *sits back down. They wait.*

JUDITH. Where did you put... William?

SAMUEL. In the barn.

JUDITH. Did you... cover his face with something?

SAMUEL. A bit of sack. More than he deserves.

Pause.

JUDITH. We should have buried him and said that he'd vanished.

SAMUEL. No. I told you. We've nothing to hide.

JUDITH. You killed him, Sam.

SAMUEL. Aye, I did. And I'm proud of it.

Pause.

We should get a reward, for what we've done. Compensation.

JUDITH. You're not going to say that.

SAMUEL. I am. They sent him into our house. A fox in the shape of a boy.

JUDITH. Don't say that. Call him a collaborator. And don't get angry. That won't help.

WILLIAM. He says he's come to help, really he's come to try and finish us off, because his friends couldn't do for us in March!

JUDITH. When the foxfinders get here –

SAMUEL. I'll have a few choice words for them.

JUDITH. We've got to explain it, calmly. We've got to make them understand, or…

SAMUEL. I'll tell them all right. How he didn't want to search the farm properly. Kept making excuses. Didn't want to go to the woods, because he knew that was where they were hiding.

JUDITH. He ignored the sign. The message in the wool. Don't forget to say that.

SAMUEL. Aye, that's right.

JUDITH. What else?

SAMUEL. He said he couldn't see the foxes in the woods, when they were right there, right in front of him!

JUDITH. He tried to stop you from shooting at them.

SAMUEL. Aye. Didn't follow me when I chased them. And when you came… he attacked you. I'd had my doubts, but that's when I knew. I saw the beast in him.

Pause.

We ought to be compensated. It's not right, what happened.

JUDITH. What if they don't believe us?

SAMUEL. Course they will. It's the truth, isn't it?

There's a knock at the door.

The End.

A Nick Hern Book

Foxfinder first published in Great Britain as a paperback original in 2011 by Nick Hern Books Limited, 14 Larden Road, London W3 7ST, in association with Papatango and the Finborough Theatre, London

Foxfinder copyright © 2011 Dawn King

Dawn King has asserted her right to be identified as the author of this work

Cover image: Garry Lake www.garrylakephotography.com
Cover design: Ned Hoste, 2H

Typeset by Nick Hern Books, London
Printed in Great Britain by Mimeo Ltd, Huntingdon, Cambridgeshire PE29 6XX

A CIP catalogue record for this book is available from the British Library

ISBN 978 1 84842 244 5